QUEST FOR HARMONY
IN
ROMEN BASU'S NOVELS

QUEST FOR HARMONY
IN
ROMEN BASU'S NOVELS

G.R. Malliga

Facet Books International
New York

First published in India 1998

Publishers
Facet Books International
345 East 69th Street
New York 10021, USA

ISBN 0-9323-7771-8

Phototypeset in Palatino 11pt by
Tara Chand Sons
Naraina, New Delhi - 110028

Printed at
D.K. Fine Art Press Pvt. Ltd.
Ashok Vihar, Delhi

Contents

Preface

Romen Basu as a living author has published twelve
novels. He also has three short story collections and four
volumes of poems to his credit. He has concentrated on
joint family system in his earlier novels and his later novels centre around social problems. His style is simple while
his statements are sharp and emphatic. His themes are
complex and the social problems which constitute the
themes are caste, religion and class. The theme or 'cause',
as he calls it, calls for attention and study.

Romen Basu hails from an aristocratic Bengali
family. His literary heritage can be traced to his grand-
father Jogindra Basu, a poet laureate. He has served the
United Nations Organization for forty years. During his
career he has worked on several projects to establish world
peace. His profession has taken him around the world several times and his experiences have added to his sphere of
knowledge. He began his literary career late in his life and
all his earlier experiences contribute to the human understanding as reflected in the novels. He writes mostly about
India and publishes his works in India though his novels
are popular in America. His frequent visits to India keep
him informed of the current socio-political and economic
affairs.

As a person, born and brought up in a joint family, he
is aware of the merits and demerits of the system of joint
living. His boyhood experiences provide him with mate-

rial for the first novel *A House Full of People*. As a man he is aware of the fact that the degeneration of joint family system is a threat to the happiness of the family life. The novel shows a life picture of a joint household. The author also exposes the shortcomings of the joint family system such as exploitation of the eldest son and elder brother, the hierarchy in the family, lack of freedom for younger generation. The researcher's hypothesis is that the unconscious support for the joint family system runs as an undercurrent in his novels though he presents the merits and demerits of the system without any bias. However, his obvious support for the joint family for the values as seen in the novels is confirmed by his interview with the researcher.

The Western education, industrialization and urbanisation have resulted in disintegration of families. The Indians, aping the Western culture, disregard the joint family system, which Basu disapproves of. Basu is neither orthodox nor tradition-bound in recommending the joint family system. He sincerely feels that joint family is suitable to the Indian condition. The demerits in the joint family system are overruled by the merits and the demerits can be rectified, if necessary. He approves of the hierarchy operating at the familial level because the family benefits by it. At the same time he argues against the hierarchy in the society because it leads to oppression and exploitation. He feels sorry for the lower classes and their 'cause' forms the theme for many of his later novels.

The Indian society which is steeped in religion blindly accepts anything in the name of religion. The factors that divide the society — caste, class and gender — function mainly with the religious sanction. Romen Basu instead of superficially dealing with the aspects of stratification probes into the origin of the social menace. He believes that religion is responsible for dividing the society in the guise of caste, class and gender. As a sensitive citizen and a good artist Basu responds to the social injustice and this study tries to examine the novels of Basu with a view to providing the right perspective on Basu.

Romen Basu is an Indian and an Internationalist at the same time. With a thorough knowledge about the Indian superstitions and sentiments, he writes about the Indian societies which are bound by religion. All the same, his knowledge of world cultures and cross-cultures directs him to take an aerial view of the Indian ethos.

The protest element in his fight for the 'cause' is rather meek in his early works. Gradually his response becomes more emotional and expressive. In his latest novel one can see a comprehensive understanding of the human mind and society. From the microcosm of the family to the macrocosm of the society and Universe, the author's wish for a harmonious living is ostensible. The 'cause' is the cause that deters peace and he champions this cause of the underdogs to wipe out all the disturbing elements in the quest for peace and harmony. The study takes up for close analysis the growth of the writer at various stages as reflected in the novels. The 'cause' is also studied under the light of the ways and means for universal peace.

The introductory chapter traces the growth of the Indian English novel with the special emphasis on sociological novelists. The history of Indian English novels includes the British rule in India, freedom struggle, independence and partition because the impact of political upheavals can be felt in the creations during those times. Romen Basu appears on the arena when the Indian English novel has widened its sphere with psychological and sociological dimensions. How Romen Basu is unique in his treatment of the sociological problems is discerned. His commitment to his subject and themes is dealt with. The life of the novelist and a brief summary of all his novels is furnished. The quest for harmony on the part of the writer at two levels — family and society — is examined.

The second chapter "Familial Amity" focuses the early novels which centre around joint family system. As a person who is brought up in a joint family Romen Basu presents a life-like picture of the family. The merits and demerits are pictured without any prejudice. However, the unconscious support for the joint family can be gleaned. The author is neither sentimental nor orthodox in recommending the joint family system. His international experience only affirms his preference. He is aware of the fact that nuclear families in Western countries have only resulted in estrangement and alienation. The exploitation and oppression of the younger generation in the name of religion and caste is highlighted while he is optimistic that this can be rectified. Familial harmony need not be an illusion and Romen Basu's sincere effort to achieve the harmony is arrived at in this chapter.

The third chapter "Societal Discordance" throws light on the widening of the perspective of the novelist from family to society. The author who tolerates the hierarchy in the society for obvious reasons argues against the hierarchy in the family. This response which is mild in his earlier novels becomes forceful in his later novels. In this growth, the author's reaction from passive statements to vehement remarks is traced with reference to his novels. The author finally shows endurance and complacence in the later novels, establishing the quest for harmony. The author's commitment to the social issues is explored. The author's effort to probe into the root cause of the problem awakens him to the fact that religion forms an important and strong force in the life of Indian mind. The unquestioning faith in religion leads the Indian people to the many evils of the society. This chapter studies the author's ideas in a sociological perspective.

The fourth chapter "Art as Technique" shows the artist in the author, defends him against the popular opinion that he is a Marxist and Communist. The requirements of

the Marxist writer are furnished with the view to distinguish Romen Basu from the Marxian novelists. The stylis-
tic features of the writer are scrutinized with the aspects of
the novel in focus. Romen Basu's ability as a novelist is
thus proved. The technique of placing the individual against
the society and vice versa is dealt with. The interaction
between the individual and society as a never ending phenomenon and the novelist's effort to use it for his purpose
is expounded. The factors that operate against the individuals are many and those who fight for changes in the
society put up with the onslaughts. Some individuals are
victims while some others are victorious. The chapter
exemplifies the individuals in Basu's novels and the
society's response to them.

The fifth and final chapter sums up the quest for harmony at the universal level. Romen Basu as an Indian and
world citizen exhibits a wide sphere of knowledge and
understanding in his approach to problems in life. Being a
living novelist, he shows bright prospects for further
research.

The novelist as a man and as an artist is thus established. Moreover the novelist's interview confirms the ideas
that appear in the novels which is a testimony to his commitment. The novelist's facility in treating complex issues
such as sex and man-woman relationship is commended.
The consistency of his ideas and themes in relation
with his interview is juxtaposed to highlight the novelist's
integrity.

G.R. Malliga

Chapter 1
Introduction

The novel is the one bright book of life. Books are not life. They are only tremulations on the ether. But the novel as a tremulation can make the whole man alive tremble.

(D.H. Lawrence "Why the novel matters" 133)

The 'novel', one of the major and most effective forms of literature, often reflects life, thereby becoming an expression of society. The novelist through the medium of language establishes a relationship between the writer and the reader. This relationship is mutual because both the writer and the reader are members of the society. Fiction, a "...modern counterpart to epic" (K. Chellappan "Voice in Exile: Journey in Raja Rao and V.S. Naipaul" 25), provides a comprehensive view and scrutiny of the genre and society. By its very nature it commands a widespread audience. Its accessibility, simplicity and intelligibility have made the novel celebrated, though this genre is a comparatively recent phenomenon. In addition to the delight the novel renders, it has also a social function. It becomes an effective tool in the hands of the social reformers. The novelists become social reformers when their artifacts bring about transformation in the socio-political and economic spheres.

The impact of the novel on the society is significant. Hippolyte Taine is not beside the point when he says, "Literature is the consequence of the race, moment and the *milieu*" (quoted in Wilbur Scott *Five Approaches* 123). But it is equally true that "The writer is not only influenced by society: he influences it. Art not merely reproduces life but also shapes it" as Wellek and Warren put it (*Theory of Literature* 102). Harry Levin explicates this relationship between literature and society succinctly: "The relations between Literature and Society are reciprocal. Literature is not only the effect of social causes, it is also the cause of social effects" (quoted in S. Ravindranathan *Principles of Literary Criticism* 99).

This dictum can very well be applied to Indian English literature that has emerged as an independent literature from the roots of English literature. Its growth is due to the consequence of the British regime and the Indian response to it. In the West, the growth of the novel is associated with the emergence and growth of the middle class. It may be in the fitness of things here to have a brief survey of some of the Indian English literature over the last several decades with special reference to the sociological writers. The backwardness of Indian social conditions has induced social reformers like Raja Ram Mohan Roy to publish articles on contemporary problems and social evils. After the initial phase of drafting pamphlets, articles and reviews, Indians begin to exhibit a literary sensibility in English. This sensibility coupled with social awareness paves the way for Indian novel in English. Bankim Chandra Chatterjee's *Rajmohan's Wife*, the first Indian novel in English, discusses the sad plight of Indian women. His other works are equally emphatic of the same theme, including widow remarriage. The Hindu society and the joint family system with all the defects are dealt with in other works. The social life of India with all its vagaries has provided themes and material for novelists such as A.S.P. Ayyar, K.S. Venkatramani, and Romesh Chandra Dutt to weave

patterns for their creative fiction. D.V.K. Raghavacharyulu
traces this process:

> The Indo-Anglian pen was employed in the battle
> of wits and in the collision of arguments and per-
> spectives with a simple urgency commensurate with
> the new-won power of an expressive resource. The
> process has continued, with the result that it over-
> laps the next successive phases. From Vivekananda
> to Aurobindo, from Raja Ram Mohun Roy to
> Tagore, from Tilak, Gokhale, and Gandhi to Nehru,
> Radhakrishnan and Rajaji, the Indian writers of En-
> glish prose have been primarily concerned with the
> exploration of thought on a level of stylistic em-
> piricism rather than with the pursuit of vision on
> the level of creative imagination.

(Critical Essays on Indian Writing in English 340)

Among the living Indian English writers being
researched, Romen Basu the study of whose fiction has
been taken for the present study is unique in more than
one sense. The fact that his sensibility is genuinely Indian
combining with an international experience makes him a
writer of sociological novels with a fair sense of objectivity.
He provides a synthesis for sociological novel with equal
concentration on psychological dimensions. The Marxian
undertones merge with feministic outburst to bring out the
artist in Romen Basu. While the other novelists expose the
social malignancy superficially, Romen Basu delves deep
into the origin of the social evils. His commitment to the
social problems makes him extraordinary among Indian
writers. As a sensitive and rational writer, he presents the
problems without any fear or hesitation, which makes him
a class by himself.

Romen Basu is a writer of international reputation. It
is strange that he has not drawn the attention of the Indian
critics as much as the other Indian English writers. This
researcher attempts to compensate for that lacuna to some
extent. So far many book reviews have appeared, mostly

in foreign journals. During the researcher's interview, Romen Basu informed the researcher that a full length study is yet to be published. Among the articles that have appeared, K.T. Krishna Prasad's "Romen Basu: An Introduction" is worth mentioning. The credit of introducing Romen Basu to Indian readers can be attributed to him.

D.S. Rao's elaborate book review on the novel *Portrait on the Roof* studies the diverse elements — East-West encounter, characterization, and joint family system. Ayyappa Panicker praises Basu's short stories. Meera Bose's review on *Outcast* published in *Literary Criterion* expounds the theme of the novel including the literary merits. To complimented by another novelist is noteworthy and Mu Raj Anand's review of the novel *Sands of Time* apprecia. Romen Basu for his endeavour. Anand traces the bureau cracy and political views of the United Nations. The di culty of mingling politics and fiction is also acknowledged. Ravindranathan studies *Outcast* and *Blackstone* from a sociological perspective. The journals such as *Patriot*, *Statesman*, and *Literary Criterion* and newspapers such as *The Hindu*, *National Herald* published reviews of Romen Basu's books. He deserves a deep study and hence the researcher's attempt.

Romen Basu was born in 1923 in Calcutta in India. He belongs to the community of Kayasthas. He grew up in a joint family consisting of sixty-five members. His uncles were doctors, professors, solicitors and barristers and Basu's father was the only businessman who made considerable economic uplift. The eldest uncle sweated his blood to feed the sixty-five members while the other uncles did not contribute a nickel to the family maintenance. In addition to providing food and shelter Basu's uncle gave them education and all comforts including cars, servants, picnics, etc. Basu's great-grandfather Kabi Bhusan Jogindernath Basu began his career as a school teacher, became a Headmaster, a Professor and then poet.

Romen Basu completed his undergraduate course in Economics. He studied Charter Secretaries in London and Masters in Business Administration in the United States of America. He joined the government of India service in England. He was appointed the Assistant Private Secretary to the Indian High Commissioner V.K. Krishna Menon. Later he joined the United Nations in 1948 and dedicated thirty-five years in career service and five more years as a consultant co-ordinator of the Lumbini project. He began his literary career late in life but he has not given a break ever since.

In addition to Basu's professional and literary career, he had worked as the Chief of the Office of Under Secretary General for DTCD. He had been a staff activist and Presiding Officer of the Staff Council and had been the Secretary of the Board as well. He has spent five years in Thailand on field assignment and served on the Economic Commission for Asia and Far East. He had worked on the Mekong project for three years and served as UNDP assistant resident representative in Libya. He was the Secretary of the Board of Trustees of United Nations' International School. He has visited one hundred and twenty countries and his commissions had taken him around the globe every year.

Regarding Basu's writing career he had been writing only on the subjects of economic development in the beginning. Literary influence came in his mid forties when Christine Weston, author of *Indigo*, simply asked him to sit down and write. He cites various authors as formative influence on him including Russians, Japanese, of whom he has read in translation. He runs a publishing house Facet Books International to promote Indian authors. He has been reading Indian newspapers regularly to keep abreast of the Indian social and political situation. His visits to the Golden Temple after the Operation Blue Star to gather news for his novel *My Own Witness* prove his sincerity and commitment. When he was touring Midnapore with his daughter who was working on women's protest, he hit upon the plot for his novel *Outcast*.

Romen Basu seems to have used his spare hour to his advantage. In the midst of a heavy schedule in the United Nations he pursued his writing career. To quote him on his creativity: "...my writing career began literally on the drawing board. Wherever I could snatch five minutes' time in trains, subways, buses and most of all during air travels I opened the writing pad. The first result of my effort was a manuscript of *A House Full of People*" (Romen Basu, lecture at Tirunelveli 20.03.1993). The novel saw publication after two years and he has not stopped writing since that day.

The chief influence on Basu's literary career is the 'cause' he wants to champion. He is able to find burning issues compelling him to write. He believes that fiction is a human document and that as it involves writing about human concerns, foibles and vicissitudes of life, it bears a semblance to reality. The choice of medium of language evokes a determined reply: "I do submit that there is no room for parochialism or nationalism in the matter of language. Every language is a universal language. Any language in which an author chooses to write is his personal preference" [lecture].

The writers experience slack periods and peak periods in their writing careers. They often await the visits of the Muse. Basu reports that the Muse visits him daily for there is no fluctuation in his creativity. Regarding the formative influences, he acknowledges that in the initial period there was no literary influence excepting the Gandhian truth and Buddha's writings. He admires and appreciates Kawabata, Tolstoy, Faulkner, Howard Fast, Hemingway, Saul Bellow, Naruda, Sarat Chandra, Michael and Madhusudan Dutt. The English translations of Japanese literature have also come under his scrutiny and study. His travels and his acquaintance with world literature have been responsible for his universal outlook.

The family is yet another favourable influence on Basu. His wife is a lawyer who has served in the United Nations Organisation. She has been his source of inner strength: "My wife is such an understanding woman. I have not portrayed my wife in a single character but her virtues are in every woman I present" (Romen Basu, Interview with the researcher 19.03.1993). His two daughters are researchers married to American Professors. The whole family contributes to his literary career. When answering the question about the method of writing he refers to the participation of his family: "I revise two times and then give it to my wife and daughters because their comments are most valuable to me" (Interview). A writer is impelled by his own reasons for writing. Jean Paul Sartre says why a man writes:

> Each one has his reasons: for one, art is a flight; for another, a means of conquering. But one can flee into hermitage, into madness, into death. One can conquer by arms. Why does it have to be *writing*, why does one have to manage his escapes and conquests by *writing*? Because behind the various aims of authors, there is deeper and more immediate choice which is common to all of us.
>
> ("Why write?" 371)

Romen Basu's emotional reply when questioned about reasons for his writing is spontaneous:

> "My causes are social causes. My causes for the underprivileged. I stand for the cause of minority. Minority in any context. Not only the poor but when mankind suffers my heart is always for the sufferer." (Interview)

The cause does not make Romen Basu a propagandist because the artist in him excels and his cause blends with his art, turning a sociological document into a work of art.

Romen Basu made his debut with *A House Full of People* (1968) which narrates the life of a Bengali joint family. The prestigious Roy family shows fissures as the novel begins and the subsequent events show how the fissures widen into cracks and the family finally disintegrates into several nuclear families. The presentation of the feuds and bickerings within the family makes the novel life-like and lively. The plot is simple and the theme of generation gap runs as an undercurrent of the novel. The author's first hand experience might have provided the infrastructure for this novel.

Canvas and the Brush (1971) is a short story collection which consists of fascinating short stories of myriad themes. In *Your Life to Live* (1972) the hero Ashoke meets Zarina in Vienna. They marry in America against the wishes of both their families. The male-chauvinism and jealousy of Ashoke interfere in the happiness of the couple. They return to India to Ashoke's family with a hope for a better life. Zarina wins back the love of her antagonistic parents. They drift apart and Zarina lives with her parents and Ashoke with his. After a separation they realise that they really love each other. Their reunion paves way for a happier life.

A Gift of Love (1974) is a search for love by the protagonist Sukumal Ghosh. It is written in the first person narrative. The hero's free movement with all classes is resented by all his family members including his father. He indulges in undesirable activities. He runs away from home and finds his way to London in a ship. His search for love is a never ending process in which he meets Nell and Shirley in England. Shirley is a prostitute who loves him sincerely. Her untimely death shakes him and this calamity brings him back to India. He falls in love with Indu, another prostitute. His attachment to lower classes is obvious in his love affairs. Finally he marries Kajali, the servant's daughter. A careful reading of this novel establishes the fact that Sukumal lends himself for psychological interpretation.

Romen Basu attempts serious themes such as untouchability and casteism in *The Tamarind Tree* (1975). Biren, a foreign-returned engineer, loves Mohamaya, far below his status. Biren's father discourages this marriage. Mohamaya, an independent country-bred girl, shows a fine blend of intellectuality and innocence. The marriage takes place amidst obstacles. Mohamaya detests the city life and returns to Balavpur soon to be followed by Biren.

The theme of East-West encounter is conspicuous in *Candles and Roses* (1978). Samir, a married man, falls in love with a Parisian, Monique. When she comes to know of his marital status, she experiences shock but her love wins. They enjoy life till Samir's wife Pramila arrives at Paris. Samir is least perturbed by his wife's arrival because he feels no guilt about his extra-marital affair. He provides all comforts for his wife without letting down his love Monique. There is much talk about religion and philosophy. Pramila wins Samir through her penance and patience.

The next novel *Portrait on the Roof* (1980) presents a Bengali joint family which opposes the inter-religious marriage of Dilip and Teresa, an Italian. They meet in London and fall in love. He returns to India and lives an unsettled life. His love of Teresa drives him to Vienna where they settle the religious differences before uniting in wedlock.

The short story collection *Rustling of Many Winds* (1982) covers a wide range of subjects and places. His intuitive grasp of different cultures and keen ear for dialogue vivify the scenes. The anti-climax is a special feature of his short stories.

Sands of Time (1985) is a treatise of the United Nations Organisation intertwined with a feeble story of a Jew Tamara. Tamara's marriage with Ustum suffers because of her excessive Jewish sensitivity. They separate and she marries Bill. The issues of colonialism, imperialism and civil wars cover the major part of the novel. The racial discriminations and victimization of the Jewish clan are revealed through the character of Tamara.

Romen Basu's *magnum opus, Outcast* (1986), is placed in the middle of his artistic career. With this novel, Basu moves from the microcosm of the family to the macrocosm of the society. *Outcast* is a thoroughly sociological novel in which Sambal, the hero, witnesses his father being assaulted by the upper caste people for stepping into the Kali temple. His resentment over the treatment meted out to his father and his thirst for vengeance grow with him. He joins the communist party to stand against the upper class people. All his efforts to unite the lower classes end in a fiasco. The love story of Putki and Sambal is infused with the heavy social theme. Sambal relinquishes Putki in favour of his mission and Putki commits suicide. The novelist depicts an unbiased picture of the events.

Hours Before Dawn (1988) begins with the twenty-fifth wedding anniversary celebrations of Mrinal and Kabita and moves backwards — their courtship, marriage and the married life. Mrinal, a journalist, is attracted to Kabita, a doctor in London. They marry in London with the consent of their families. The marriage suffers from no obvious reason other than Kabita's soft corner for a young boy Subhas. The couple do not break the ice and Mrinal leaves for Vietnam and then to Burgundy on different assignments. The twenty-fifth anniversary brings them together but fails to unite their hearts.

Another novel of victimization and rebellion is *Blackstone* (1989). Kalapathor, a low class man, witnesses the brutal killing of his father. This event leaves indelible impression on him as a young boy. The Naxalite party uses him for their own purposes, to wipe away the zamindars. Kesab, the party leader, is an enthusiast while the chairman holds different views. The students of the University and College join the rebellion and sacrifice their lives. The love story of Kalapathor and Sabitri is a feeble sub-plot. Kalapathor quits the party because the party does not fulfil his aims. He joins Kesab and the tribal leader to form a new party. The party allegiance and party politics form the skeleton of this novel.

Reflections (1989) is a short story collection edited by Romen Basu. One of his short stories "The Feminist" finds a place in the collection. Others are replete with diverse themes.

Romen Basu continues with the sociological theme in *The Street Corner Boys* (1992). The friendship of Ghonu and Tarun suffers because of their class disparity. The political scene of this story is the second world war followed by the civil disobedience movement, communal strife and partition. The author seems to have hopes for better future because caste restrictions are not rigid as depicted in his previous novels. There is reasonable mingling between class and caste. Ghonu and Tarun continue to be close associates even after Ghonu wins elections. The women are highly independent and participate in social activities. The novel ends *cul-de-sac* leaving the reader to imagine for himself.

Basu's latest novel *My Own Witness* (1993) deals with social, political and racial injustices. Unlike the other novels limited to Bengali families, this novel speaks of a Sikh family. The theme of this novel is the 'cause' of the minority. Onkar Singh, the hero, is deeply wounded by the desecration of the Golden Temple by the Indian army. In his attempt to find out the real cause behind this cruelty, he turns a mystic. Onkar feels that all religions preach alike but the people are responsible for the factions in the society. Onkar Singh is punished with death sentence because he denies the knowledge of the real assassin. To him, integrity is more important than his own life. The author shows tolerance and maturity in his treatment of the theme and the growth of the author is discernible.

Even a cursory glance at Romen Basu's novels will reveal the fact that he wishes for harmony in family and society. So he analyses all the discordant elements in society and family. In both the spheres — caste, religion and class stand in the way of creating concordant atmosphere. The Indian society which is highly religious accepts everything that is done and said in the name of religion. The caste and the caste hierarchy as approved by the religion divides the family and the children leave their homes for marriage options. Romen Basu aims at harmony among these divisions. The caste system and class division are acceptable to him as they were in their origins, which denote only various ways of living. He hopes for an ideal society where the different elements can work complementarily. In the family too his arguments are placed in favour of the peaceful functioning of the family which this study highlights.

The empowerment may lead to exploitation and suffering in a hierarchy when power lies with the people at the apex. Any reformist or propagandist will protest against the centralisation of power and authority. But Basu is different. Romen Basu's ways and means are unique because he intends to bring about disagreeable elements into agreement. He ignores the centralisation of power with the head of the family as far as family is concerned—considering the values involved. But, he raises arms against similar inequalities in the society owing to their harmful nature.

The earlier novels of Romen Basu centre around the joint family system with which the author is familiar. Basu depicts the nuances of collective living with all its advantages and disadvantages. Except the last novel all the novels picture only Bengali joint families. In his earlier novels Romen Basu treads on familiar grounds by presenting upper middle class joint families. Hence, the realistic picture. The nobility of the head of the family is not only exclusive to Bengali joint family but a universal factor and Basu portrays it with grandeur and magnanimity. The author believes in the success of the joint family because of the security it can give to the family members. The disintegration of the joint family in the Indian soil can be attributed to industrialisation, urbanisation and western education.

Indians, by aping the western culture, have done away with joint families, the epitome of a rich cultural heritage. The author, a non-resident, still feels that Indian joint family is meritorious despite a few demerits. One can feel that the author disapproves of nuclear families in support of joint family. He weaves themes of romance, love, religion, friendship around the main axis of the joint family.

After pleading for harmony at the micro level — at the family scene, Basu extends his landscape — making the society as the backdrop for his fiction. Romen Basu widens his perspective, extending his focus to the society after the initial phase of the family. The society — with all its divisions of caste, class and religion — forms the subject in his later novels. Basu who advocates joint family system by overlooking its demerits inveighs against the caste hierarchy because the stratification is harmful to the society. This approach is a unique feature in his novels, worthy of approbation. His unbiased treatment of the social issues distinguishes him from other novelists.

A Bengali by birth and an internationalist by choice and attitude, one can find Romen Basu to be a versatile artist. His wide experience has shaped him into a tolerant observer. His minute observation naturally blends with the story to make history without footnotes. The Indianness of Romen Basu is evident when he paints Indian scenes in words. His plea for the familial harmony is sincere and poetic. While many Indian writers try to ape western culture in the form of nuclear family, Basu is interested in upholding the joint family system, which is slowly dying out. What is interesting is his international experience — especially his life at the western countries has all the more convinced him of the merits of the joint family system which provides familial harmony. How he presents his case for familial harmony through the joint family system is the concern of the next chapter.

Chapter 2
Familial Amity

Friendship does not give security. Relations do not give that security which family does. As you cry with the family, you share the joys and sorrows with the family and that joy I can understand because I live everyday with it. It is the most beautiful experience that has happened to me.

(Romen Basu Interview with the researcher
19.03.1993)

As a conscientious artist Romen Basu is a crusader for harmony. In his quest for harmony he faces extreme situations. One is social injustice which is a major threat to communal harmony. With all the tall talk about 'national integration', 'secularism' and 'unity in diversity', Indians are divided among themselves into various groups in terms of caste and religion.

However, for the tradition-bound Basu, what is more sickening is the disintegration of the joint family system. All the western experiences convince him of the nobility of the joint family which is gradually dying under the influence of the western culture.

The joint family system is a common feature of the Indian society. Generally, a family consists of two or more generations living together in harmony and agreement. Usually the members of the same family, i.e., sons of the same parents, their spouses and children constitute a joint family. Sometimes distant relatives become a part of the family. The eldest member of the family shoulders the family responsibilities and decides on investments, expenditure, marriage, education and all matters relating to the family. The whole family accepts the headship without questioning. Besides the head of the family, all the elders are respected and the hierarchy is acknowledged.

This type of a joint family has centralised power and authority. The head of the family is supposed to be and in most cases remains traditional and orthodox. The freedom of the younger generations suffers to some extent owing to the restrictions and customs of the joint family. The household enforces rules and regulations on matters of dress and food. It exercises control over their behaviour and activities. Any challenge to the authority or any act that may even remotely tarnish the reputation of the family is not tolerated.

In the joint family or extended family as it is known, the male authority is predominant. The wife of the head of the family has authority only over the domestic side of the household such as cooking, organizing and co-ordinating the activities of other women and managing the servants. She also trains the female children for the further maintenance of the household. The girls are taught to cook, sew, sing and perform other feminine activities while the boys are encouraged to study and play games. The distinction between male and female is strictly followed.

The family consciousness in Indian societies is intense and obvious. The members of the joint family work for the welfare and reputation of the family. The contribution of all the members results in successful functioning of the family. This structure of the family pivots on love and affection among the family members. Karve defines a joint family as "...a group of people who generally live under one roof, who eat food cooked at one hearth, who hold property in common and who participate in common family worship and are related to each other as some particular type of kindred" (*Kinship Organisation in India* 10). Karve thus reveals the major characteristics of the joint family.

The Indian economy has until recently depended basically on agriculture which requires a rudimentary specialisation of labour. The environment has paved way for a stable way of life with tradition and custom as the dominant features. Such an environment provided ideal setting for the joint family to thrive and such families give a feeling of security to every individual.

Romen Basu's personal preference for the family arises out of deep contemplation. He feels that the harmony in the family can give the sense of security which is absent from the culture of the west where people live in nuclear families. The familial harmony paves way for the universal harmony and Romen Basu tries to inculcate this idea in the minds of his readers. His viewpoint finds expression in the following words: "I can give my perception of why I recommend it because the joint family gives you that sense of security which nothing ever can. Apart from the fact, the nuclear family lowers your standard and you become selfish and dehumanized when you tear yourselves away" (Interview).

A House Full of People, Basu's first novel, portrays a Bengali joint family in exactitude. With a thorough knowledge and understanding Romen Basu depicts his characters catering to the requirements of a large household. The Roy family in *A House Full of People* is proud of its long pedigree. The family consists of nearly sixty members including relatives. Sudhin Roy, the head of the family, takes care of the relatives who would have been orphans otherwise. Ranjith speaks in approbation of Sudhin Roy's generosity in supporting the poor relations:

> Grandmother's penniless widowed sister would say
> that if she had not come to live with us here, she
> would have had to resort to begging. Father's sister's

> two sons would say that if they did not have this
> place to live in, it would have been impossible for
> them to go to college. (68)

The large family, as characterized by Basu, shows intimacy
and mutual assistance in times of need, without which the
joint family cannot succeed for long.

There is yet another instance in *A House Full of People*
which demonstrates the nobility of the joint family system.
Reba is engaged to be married but Saral, her father, is hard
up for money. Sudhin Roy, the head of the family, realises
the difficulty of his brother Saral and divides the marriage
expenditure among all brothers in proportion to their income. He himself accepts the major share of expenditure.
Saral knows that he could not have managed on his own
and feels grateful to his elder brother for helping him out
of difficulty. When Anil, another brother, shows reluctance
in contributing his share Sudhin points out:

> No one can force you to contribute anything to
> your niece's wedding. Just remember that none of
> us have all the money to get our girls married. I
> know your girl is still young, but her turn will come.
> Also don't think we are asking for charity. Every
> penny will be paid back. (79)

Every member willingly or unwillingly participates in the
work. They rise to the occasion to retrieve the person from
any entanglement. The joint family paves way for taking
the load off one's shoulder by sharing it among the family
members.

Kamala in *Portrait on the Roof* gratefully remembers
her brother Bholanath who supports her family in times of
need. But for the monetary help of Bholanath, all her sons
would have turned vagabonds. The narration reveals the
pathetic condition of the family:

> It was not easy to take care of fourteen children
> with an uncertain income that depended on good

> rains. How many Saturdays had her elder brother
> not driven out to her home in the wilderness to
> deliver bags of rice, tins of kerosene and packets of
> sugar and in the malaria season quinine and nour-
> ishing food. Where else would she have found
> shelter for her entire family for a whole year? (8)

The kinship is maintained by benevolence and the inhabitants are bound by love and affection. This security that the
family provides cannot be equalled with wealth, power or
fame.

An anecdote from a short story of Romen Basu "Touch
Me" will be relevant in this context, wherein he juxtaposes
the Indian and western cultures. Tim, an American, takes
to drugs because of the divided family and loveless life.
His penpal Jathumal invites him to India to join his family.
Tim narrates his infant days to Jathumal: "When I was five
years old, sometimes I had trouble reaching my bed from
the door, plowing through a mountain of toys. I remember
that very well, but I don't remember if I ever slept under
the same blanket with my mother" (*Rustling of Many Winds*
34). A feeling of insecurity and isolation grips the westerners
because of divided families. What is significant here is the
question of values. To get married into a large family is
considered good and secure in India. Mechanization and
materialistic attitude of the west are slowly finding their
way into India and one may discern the trend in recent
times of a sharp decline in the preference for joint living.
The craving for the family by Tim signifies the values of
the family.

It becomes natural that the large households feel proud
of the family heritage, caste, wealth, education and social
status. The goodwill of the family is considered an asset
and nurtured with pride. Prabha, one of the daughters-in-
law of the Roy family, tells Chaya:

> When my father married me into this family, he
> said just one thing. He could have found me a

richer husband and a wealthier home where I could have been comfortably off for the rest of my life but he was not looking for that because money is not everything in life. He stressed that in this family there would be culture and my children would grow up with the right values.

(*A House Full of People* 14)

The reputation of the family is guarded with utmost care by all the members which means acceptance of restrictions and rigidity in their way of life. The honour of the family is maintained by adhering to the rules of the society.

Any impediment to the honour in the form of inter-caste or inter-religious marriages is not permitted because the prestige of the family suffers. Sukumal, the hero of *A Gift of Love*, decides to marry the daughter of the servant-maid. This marriage outside the caste and the class is resented by the whole family. The family is more worried about its reputation. Sukumal's brother shouts at him accusing him for the disgrace to the family honour:

What about our colleagues in the profession? They would avoid us as lepers. The neighbours won't even spit in front of our house every time they passed by. The relatives won't come even for Bijoya's *pronam*. You are a scoundrel of the worst type. You should be horsewhipped. You should be thrashed from head to toe. You are a disgrace to society, a disgrace to the human race. (175)

Romen Basu is aware of the unwritten laws of the society. He weaves his plots and characters without comments, maintaining an aesthetic distance with a sense of understanding and tolerance.

The Tamarind Tree shows the 'class' to be the obstacle in Biren's marriage. Biren loves Mohamaya who is far above his caste and below in class. Biren's father Anukul is unwilling to permit the wedding to take place in Mohamaya's place even though Mohamaya is a Brahmin and higher than their caste. The class difference shows up when he says: "Are you suggesting that guests in my son's wedding will be farmers, potters, *chandals* and all those lower class people? How can you say that? Even if I reserved a train to take my guests to Balavpur, where will they sit, in the rice field" (114)? Anukul is more bothered about the audience in the wedding than his son marrying into an ordinary family. The prestige on the basis of status is maintained at any cost by the large households.

Romen Basu, an internationalist in outlook, portrays an Italian scene where the conditions seem to be no different. The conversation between Teresa and Dilip in *Portrait on the Roof* shows that the Italians are as conscious of family prestige as Indians. The conversation brings out this similarity:

> "Personally, I think lawyers in Italy have lower status than Fiat workers. The only others who are more looked down on by the people are politicians."
>
> "You cannot be serious."
>
> "The reputation of these professions is low because they are not truthful."
>
> "I see what you mean."
>
> "Father worries about all of us. For us the family is everything." (35)

If Basu presents the sentiments of the older generation without comments, the youngsters having their own way has to be interpreted carefully. Even amidst oppositions Ranjith and Chithra in *A House Full of People*, Biren and Mohamaya in *The Tamarind Tree* marry and make their marriages successful. Though as an individual, with his cosmopolitan outlook, Basu would have preferred an inter-caste or inter-religious marriage, his personal views do not find an open expression in his fiction. What he underscores here is the generation gap which leads to the slow disintegration of the joint family system. In the patriarchal or patrilineal family the crucial aspects of the family structure rest in the hierarchy of power and control. This structure may or may not be supported by the emotional elements such as sentiments, affection or respect. In the traditional large family the eldest man is in the apex of the hierarchy. On his death, authority passes to the next eldest male member. The power of the head of the family in deciding on the matters concerned with the family makes him responsible for his decisions. Romen Basu presents typical joint families in his novels. The Roy family has gathered for a definite purpose of releasing the house from mortgage. Sudhin Roy, the titular head, has mortgaged the house without the knowledge of his brothers, only for the maintenance of the family. He wishes to raise money from his brothers for releasing the mortgage, which the brothers refuse to comply with. Sudhin intervenes:

> All of you are married with three or four children each, and yet in the ten years since father's death, not one of you has contributed a penny for the maintenance of the family. Do you think it is up to me to support your wives and children for the rest of my life? Do you realize what I have to go through everyday to feed fifty mouths? Now you turn around and say that it is my fault that I mortgaged the house and it is my responsibility to get us out of the difficulty.
>
> (*A House Full of People* 6)

The power includes the responsibility and the head of the family shoulders it willingly. Sudhin's outrage finds expression only because of the lack of co-operation of his brothers.

In Sudhin's deathbed Prabha recollects all that Sudhin has done for the Roy family: "No man I know has done more for the family than you. You have supported the family since your father's death....Besides the material comforts, you have shown them kindness, charity, tolerance and understanding. If they have not learned anything from

your example it is only your fault" (*A House Full of People*
110-111). One may quote David Mandelbaum who explains
the responsibility of the head of the family:

> The grandfather was theoretically the head of the
> family until his death. This gave him power over
> his wife and children, his younger brothers and his
> sisters until they were married. Even those who
> moved away to distant cities, or overseas, were
> theoretically still members of the family and there-
> fore under his control although he could not super-
> vise their day-to-day affairs. On his death the au-
> thority passed to the next eldest male.
>
> ("The Family in India" 94)

The position of the head of the family entails much
potential power and the whole family respects the head. In
Your Life to Live Ashoke marries Zarina in America and
brings her to his house, full of people. Zarina is unfamiliar
with Bengali customs. Ashoke indicates to her that she
should touch his father's feet as a mark of respect. He
adds: "Now you are a Bengal wife. You have to show your
respect the way my father would expect it" (123). Ashoke's
faithful adherence to the customs despite his modernity
underlines his inherent cultural influence.

The crown prince or the heir to the family headship is
trained even from his boyhood. Romen Basu pictures a
scene in which Sudhin worries about Arun, the next heir
to the headship. Sudhin laments to Prabha: "He is the eldest after all. He has to carry on with the tradition and
have the responsibility of this family. How can be behave
like an upstart" (*A House Full of People* 20)?

The respect for elders is a common feature in Indian
families. The members address each other with respect.
The boys dare not smoke in front of the elders. The young
people cannot afford to come home late. Ranjith, who is
employed, comes home late tiptoeing into the house. The
dinner has been left in his room. His mother waits for him

with questions, "Are you making a habit of coming home at 11 O'clock? Do you know that your father gets furious when you are not home by dinner time" (*A House Full of People* 133)? Even grown-ups are controlled by their elders in their daily activities.

In *Your Life to Live* Ashoke briefs Zarina on the ways of life in their household in Calcutta. He also insists on following the rules after giving her instructions:

> Ashoke told Zarina not to wear anything except sarees and to keep her head covered, especially in front of the elders. He had suggested that it was not necessary for her to wear shoes or slippers as no one else did....Zarina was to eat with the ladies, sometimes joining the aunts, sometimes the cousins, depending upon what she was instructed by the eldest aunt. She learned that it was not polite to talk to Ashoke in the presence of elders. (124-125)

Unlike western families the Indian families are laws unto themselves.

Romen Basu is aware of these customs and the physical demonstration of respect in day-to-day life. Mohamaya, the heroine of *The Tamarind Tree*, finds her life suffocated by rigid routines: "Mohamaya was not to forget to keep her head covered in front of the elders. She must always attend her father-in-law at his dinner. She was not to appear on the verandah overlooking the main street when the men went to work and returned home" (130). Though obedience is thrust upon the younger generation, mostly it is accepted with willingness. In *Hours Before Dawn* Romen Basu sums up the harmonious working of the family: "It was a revelation to Kabita how well everyone got along without any dictation, each did his own thing. Miraculously it produced its own harmony. The chain of command according to hierarchy was respected. No one contradicted an elder; they disagreed but always obeyed" (60). The harmony seen in the family of Mrinal perhaps is the ideal family that Basu has in mind.

A contrasting picture of western culture, free will and independence is seen in a short story "United Parcel Service". The family portrayed in the short story is devoid of love and affection. Sandra's right wrist is almost severed from her hand for which she is admitted into the hospital. The neighbours convey this news to Sandra's mother who says, "Sandra has always been careless even when she was a child" (*Rustling of Many Winds* 56). One does not see a shock-stricken or a grieved mother. Rather one sees a formal mother who sends a bouquet of flowers and checks with the parcel service for a thank-you note. After a lapse of years when the mother is ailing the daughter returns in the same coin by sending a get-well card which reads: "In gratitude for teaching me to stand on my own two feet" (60). Independence as practised in western countries results in estrangement and alienation. The short story, by tone and moral, supports the family ideal by emphasizing the defects of the independent spirit of the west.

The women generally occupy only a secondary position in the family. The men control the financial matters while the women manage the household work and train the children. They also take charge of family worship and observe ceremonial functions. The wife of the head of the family holds authority over the organization of the work of other women. The girls are not educated like boys because they are supposed to be subservient. Romen Basu's households fit into this frame of the Indian joint family. Chaya finds fault with Sunanda for the misuse of grocery. Karan, Chaya's husband, comes to Sunanda's rescue:

> You know that she alone can run domestic affairs properly. She and she alone works hard and gets along with everybody. Except Chabi, every one of you has tried your hand at it. You could not manage for one week. The servants, the cook, the maids, everyone wanted to leave when you took over.
>
> (*A House Full of People* 74)

The household duties are considered to be woman's responsibilities. She is expected to fulfil the assigned duties without fail. The knack of housekeeping is expected in every woman and Chaya's failure is considered by her husband as a disqualification and he says so.

The domain of the woman is restricted to the home. The woman of the house in *Your Life to Live* tells Zarina about the Bengali tradition:

> We believe in tradition, a way of life where women play a subordinate role to the men. A Bengali girl is taught by the time she is twelve years old that her real aim in life is to serve her husband and obey him for the good of the family. We frown upon the modern way of life. For instance, do you know that in this house there is not one woman who has passed her matriculation examination. (129-130)

The conversation continues with convincing arguments and the lady explains the problem with the modern woman: "Frankly, I think it is bad for a woman to get too many ideas. Then they start to question everything....They begin to neglect their children. Who else but a woman keeps a home" (130)?

Romen Basu's egalitarian views may not permit him to approve of subordinate position of the woman in the family. Yet, the tradition demands it and he feels that the children brought up in such surroundings are healthier in mind and body. Perhaps Basu is able to appreciate the attitude behind such a position. The fact that women are better housekeepers, may be acceptable, if the statement is made without a gender-bias. One can consider, for instance, the Shavian Candida. She talks about her household and her husband's role in it:

> When there is money to give, he gives it: when there is money to refuse, I refuse it. I build a castle of comfort and indulgence and love for him, and

stand sentinel always to keep vulgar cares out. I
make him master here, though he does not know
it,...

("Candida" 151)

The man who is brought up in a traditional family
expects the undivided attention of his spouse. Ashoke marries outside caste and religion but expects his wife to be a
traditional woman. His male-chauvinism is revealed when
he says: "When it is about me and my wife, yes. I am the
boss in the house and I shall give you anything and everything in the whole world. My life is yours for the asking.
In return I must have your undivided, undiluted,
unashamed love and attention" (*Your Life to Live* 59).
Ashoke's attitude explains the background as to how
women came to be exploited gradually though it began as
division of labour in the familial system.

The role of the woman in the joint household is confined within the four walls of the house; nevertheless, their
responsibilities are equal to that of men. The division of
labour keeps them tethered to the house. Mohamaya, a
free and independent girl after marriage, is expected to
change her ways of life after her marriage. The negative
answer given by her baffles her in-laws. One lady among
them explains the quintessence of the role of a woman:
"The family has a tradition. A girl coming to this house
must know the basic things. We don't leave everything to
the servants" (*The Tamarind Tree* 123). Pramila in *Candles
and Roses* affirms the same idea when interviewed by a
French interviewer: "A Hindu woman is taught from birth
that she has only duties, no rights" (198). The interviewer
places the French woman in comparison with the Indian
woman: "In France, we also obey our husbands. Our joys
and sorrows, too, are inseparable from the will of our husbands. A wife will put up with everything as long as she
can feel her husband's love" (199). There is a similarity in
woman's ideas on love and marriage though the western
and eastern ideas apparently differ.

The woman's integral strength is her religion and she lives in a world of rigid moral codes. Samir tells Monique, his Parisian love, about the virtues of his wife Pramila:

> She could knit and sew, do special floral and chalk designs, and was an excellent cook and house-keeper. From the beginning she put herself at the service of his father and other members of the family. She asked only one thing for herself — that she be allowed to pray one hour each morning and two hours every evening. Words of praise spread from Shambazar to Behala how fortunate Samir's father was to have a daughter-in-law of such incomparable modesty and devotion.
>
> (*Candles and Roses* 37)

The subsidiary position of women is not resented by Romen Basu because the welfare of the family comes to the fore. The welfare of the progeny and the upkeep of the family are the fruits of the sacrifice of the womenfolk. So Basu recommends the joint family for such obvious merits.

Basu's unconscious support for the joint family system is conspicuous in his novels. Despite the bickerings and conflicts, Roy's family experiences happy moments as well. The children's requirements are attended to. Basu writes in *A House Full of People* about the prospects of a joint family:

> No crisis remained a serious matter after twenty-four hours. Everything would go back to normal and the routine of the day would be followed as usual. Sudhin looked forward to the gathering each morning at breakfast time, between seven and eight. This was his finest hour. In the enclosed verandah above the inside courtyard, exactly in front of his room, he would find all his brothers sitting on the floor, some of them still half awake and not washed. This was the hour for him to take up one by one all the domestic matters, listen to complaints, and exchange a few words with his nephews and nieces. (15)

The success of the joint family as seen in Romen Basu's novels rests on the understanding of the family members. The squabbles and feuds do not hamper the happy moments of togetherness.

In *Hours Before Dawn* Basu shows the intimate gathering of the family. Kabita and Mrinal who get married in America pay a visit to his family in Calcutta. Kabita is received with warmth and affection:

> "From the third-day, she (Kabita) became everybody's darling. The uncles wanted to talk Bengali politics with her, amazed at the interest shown in the local scene. With the young boys she talked about picnics and travel plans expecting them to show her parts of Calcutta she had not seen before. With the sisters-in-law she discussed saris and lipsticks and from the aunts she wanted recipes of the new dishes they were giving her." (58)

This happiness of getting together is totally absent in nuclear families. The interaction between the members strengthens the ties by which the familial harmony is achieved. Romen Basu aims at this harmony both in the family and the society.

A similar love of family can be cited from *Roots and Shadows* by Shashi Deshpande where she portrays a large family:

> The feeling of ease, content and indolence embraces the whole house. And the huge front door, which no child could ever push the whole way, standing wide open the whole day, so that the people just walked in and became part of the family. A feeling of welcome that didn't have to be said in words, smiles, dinners and drinks. This was home. Where one lived. Not stayed. (106)

Romen Basu and Shashi Deshpande seem to echo Robert Frost's idea:

> Home is the place where, when you have to go

there, they have to take you in!

("Death of the Hired Man" 391)

Such a home does not simply denote a place in space but a shelter where one can share joys and sorrows.

The binding element in the joint family is the inter-action with the relations. The bonds get closer the more proximal they are. The unity of the joint family has been outlined by Aileen D. Ross:

> The stability of the joint family could not be al-lowed to disintegrate because of the personal feel-ings of family members, for it was the main stable unit of the society in which it existed. The relation-ships of the various members had, therefore, to be carefully maintained and were built up through at-titudes of respect, fear, obedience and avoidance as well as love.

(*The Hindu Family in its Urban Setting* 177)

The financial matters form the main cause for rifts in the family relationships. The earners and non-earners alike en-joy the comforts and benefits which is not tolerated for a longer period. The financial problems create jealousy and petty quarrels. The members finally prefer to separate be-fore irrevocable conflicts seize the family. Sudhin in *A House Full of People* speaks of the disproportionate contributions or benefits: "How do you know whether he contributes as much as you do, do know what he contributes? Do you or anyone else, keep account of the income and the expendi-ture" (10)? The joint family is an informal structure and the financial discrepancies lead to the separation of the family. Adip, Sudhin's nephew, can no longer live in the house for similar reasons. Adip's genuine idea about the preference for joint living is:

> One accepts this situation only because of financial reasons. The only reason we live together is be-cause Jatha Sudhin supports the family. There are few people in the world like him. He is generous to

a fault. By and large, people want more than they
give and this is true even amongst brothers.

(A House Full of People 70)

The unequal contribution and lavish expenditure ruin
the family's economic structure leading to the downfall of
the family's prestige. The prestige is maintained at the
expense of the family budget. The creditor slowly acquires
the family property. When both ends do not meet, disintegration and degeneration set in. Chaya, a sensible character, argues:

> I am not at all proud. What is there to be proud of,
> to maintain a forty bedroom house, ten servants,
> two cars and all that, and not to be able to pay the
> bills? I would rather live like a poor woman within
> my means than put up this show.

(A House Full of People 13)

Romen Basu's personal experiences must have exposed
him to the cause for the crumbling of large houses. In *Your
Life to Live* there is yet another instance. Ashoke questions
the splurging on ceremonies: "To question why they had
to have thirteen religious celebrations in a year when bills
had not been paid for milk, groceries or newspapers, was
heresy. God had to be convinced by display that he was
loved and honoured, before there could be any expectation
of return" (36). The economic crisis has always been harmful to the family unity. The heavy expense of weddings,
religious festivals, lavish hospitality weigh heavily on the
family budget causing strained relationships.

Several instances of family feuds resulting from financial disparities can be cited from Romen Basu's novels. The
rhetorical questions in *Portrait on the Roof* give a new
dimension and a strong emphasis to this problem: "Did
anyone care to know how the others ate? Had the bicker-
ing ever stopped about the use of electricity or water since
these bills were paid jointly" (7)? The changing times
demand a more independent and less rigorous living which

cannot be obtained in a collective family. The younger generation tends to prefer the nuclear family system because of the disadvantages of the joint family. Romen Basu is not unaware of these drawbacks because he presents the joint families as they are.

As discussed earlier, the eldest male holds not only the highest position but heavy obligations in the traditional Hindu family. The family enjoys a prestigious position at the expense of the head of the family. He sacrifices his time, energy and money for the family's welfare. This exploitation tends to be heavily injurious to his life as Bimal says in *A House Full of People*: "What is a joint family after all? It is a form of exploitation by the younger brothers of their eldest. It encourages parasites such as these villagers from grand-father's estate who have come and settled down here" (67). Romen Basu does not vehemently condemn this exploitation because the family functions efficiently because of the sacrifice of the head of the family.

There are situations when the eldest brother has the difficulty in taking over the reins when he is not sure of his power or when a younger brother has a forceful or dashing personality. Romen Basu pictures one such situation when Sudhin in his deathbed summons all his brothers, and hands over the responsibility to Kamal although Saral is the next eldest. It is accepted by the whole family because of genuine reasons. He convinces everyone including Kamal: "I appeal to you first. You have a steady income. Please take my place. I know you feel a great deal of pride in the family. One of you will have to take charge and make the necessary sacrifices that go with it" (*A House Full of People* 118). Sudhin Roy as a head of the family is fully aware of the sacrifice that is requisite for the well-being of the family.

In addition to the sacrifice of the head of the family, his wife also has to give up her pleasures for the sake of the family. Sudhin recollects Prabha's life: "...revolved around her husband. She always anticipated what he wished and did exactly what she thought would make him happy. That meant she and her daughter sometimes had to wear rags in order to give part of the wardrobe to the one Sudhin thought needed more than his Mrs" (*A House Full of People* 111). The responsibilities tend to become irksome when heavy demands are made. If the wife of the head of the family is not willing to sacrifice, any effort by the head of the family would end in a fiasco.

Bholanath in *Portrait on the Roof* like Sudhin Roy in *A House Full of People* meets with a financial crisis: "Since Dwarakanath's death, it had been a strain for Bholanath to keep peace between the brothers and help the sister's families. He devoted more time to his family than to his career as a doctor, in which he had followed his father's footsteps" (8). Essentially, this sacrificial nature on the part of the elder brother leads to exploitation. The younger brothers revel under the sarcrifice and hard work of the elder brother. Sudhin Roy and Bholanath are embodiments of sacrifice and virtues whom the brothers try to exploit. They toil and suffer for the family and are rebuked in return. Romen Basu does not appreciate exploitation of any kind but he overlooks the exploitation on the familial level due to the overmeasuring advantages he finds in the family system. Arabindo seems to echo Romen Basu's views: "The preservation of the family is rooted in the tradition. To tamper with it is to destroy the system. The ultimate question was how much is it worth to an individual to make a sacrifice to keep the foundation intact" (*Portrait on the Roof* 24). As a well-wisher of this foundation Romen Basu does not mind the sacrifices the head of the family has to make.

Every generation differs from the previous generation in matters of food, education, lifestyle etc. One generation sometimes holds the other in contempt. While making policy decisions, friction is bound to occur. In some families this collision is destructive, resulting in the disintegration of the larger unit. The younger generation's crusade against the older generation's restrictions is a ceaseless activity. In *A House Full of People*, Arun violates the rules of the house by returning home late at nights. When his uncle Sudhin reprimands, Arun's answer comes in the form of a rebuke:

> ...your time, was your time and ours is ours. Things have changed. You cannot impose the same rules on us that were in your time. The whole outlook is old-fashioned. Even living with fifty people in the same house, eating together, sitting on the floor in a row, four or five people bathing together in open bathrooms, it's living like a flock of sheep! (21-22)

Sudhin is unable to understand the sentiments of Arun and vice versa. The generation gap is a universal phenomenon and the clash between generations is vehement in a joint family because the rules and regulations are often rigid.

Bimal, another nephew of Sudhin, feels the same way as Arun about the joint family:

> I would move out, but not for the same reason as Dada. I love my family and I am proud of them. I would be happy simply to maintain good relations with everyone and do my duty. But this old-fashioned idea of living together is not for me. Nobody is going to like, let alone, listen to another person telling them what to do.
>
> (*A House Full of People* 70)

The independence of the second generation with their option for individualistic views does not permit the dictates by the senior members.

The older generation refuses to concede to the younger in terms of respect. Anukul and Harihar are cousins who own a joint property. They quarrel over a pond and the whole village is involved in this dispute. The preservation of the family honour wins the priority and they spend a large amount of money to establish the family prestige.

The second generation does not share the preference for joint family system with their senior counterparts. They tend to feel that living together is hypocritical when the family does not really share the same sentiments. Khagen in *Portrait on the Roof* passes a critical remark about the rifts in the family: "Such idiotic claims of togetherness. Everybody in the neighbour-hood knows about their daily fights" (20). The desire to live independent lives and the love for freedom induce the younger generation to move away from their homes.

The western scene is not different in its outlook pictured in the same novel. An Italian family featuring in this novel is conscious of the family prestige like the Indian family. Uncle Umberto, a senior member of the family, understands the clash between generations: "This generation has no time for the family because other things fascinate them more. Temptation for men and women to be free with each other makes them wish to break away from the obligations of the family" (*Portrait on the Roof* 77). The generation gap is not seen exclusively in Indian families and Romen Basu projects it as a trans-cultural phenomenon in that novel. O.P. Sharma appreciates Basu's endeavour:

> The best part of the novel centres around Teresa's family presided over by her father Signor Luciano. The author gives a perceptive insight into this joint family in Italy, which has many parallels with the Mitra tribe in Calcutta where relationships are marred by family quarrels, tensions and inbuilt jealousies.
>
> (*The Tribune* 7)

The changing times have witnessed the destruction of the family system even in Europe, and the juxtaposition of the Indian and the Italian families in this novel gives a panoramic view to the idea.

Nevertheless, a writer like Jhabvala looks at family as non-individualistic phenomenon. She thinks that individuality suffers by group living. This idea is reflected in her novel, *The Nature of Passion*:

> Demure daughters-in-law, stern mother-in-law, widowed aunts, pounding spices, sifting rice and lentils, the vat of boiling milk, the barbecue, the pump in the country yard; quarrels and recriminations and occasional songs, nostalgic peasant songs or plaintive hymns winding round the ceaseless kitchen noises — these constituted the necessary, if unconsidered background to a man's life. (112)

There is subtle sarcasm in the way Jhabvala explains the daily routines in the Indian families. The scene is made to appear rustic to the western eyes. Unlike Jhabvala, Romen Basu presents laudable pictures of the joint families.

Romen Basu recommends the joint family while being conscious of its shortcomings. He personally feels that these demerits can be overridden if there is mutual tolerance. Regarding the flexibility in the family Basu answers the interviewer: "If there is some willingness of adjustment, things will work out. One who has more income must be willing to give up expecting less for himself or his family than the other to keep the institution going" (Interview).

As marriage sows seeds for the family, utmost care is paid to see that the right persons are chosen as spouses. In traditional families, the marriage partner must fit into the family pattern because life pattern differs in every family. So the elders think themselves to be in a better position to assess the prospective new member and make the choice. The privilege of choosing the life partner is not given to the people who are to get married. Any violation of these rules leads to estrangement and excommunication. Romen Basu includes several instances of conflict between the parents and children in the choice of life partners. Ranjith loves a christian girl and insists on marrying her. Ranjith's mother stubbornly rejects the proposal. In clear-cut terms she states:

> All I can say is that you will never have any per-
> mission to marry that christian girl. If you marry
> her by your own sweet will, go ahead, but you
> must leave the house. Live with your wife wher-
> ever you like, I don't want to see your wife's face.
> For me, you won't exist any more.
>
> (*A House Full of People* 135)

The marriage market in endogamous marriages as created
by the family gives much importance to the dowry and
social status. The relatives are a party to it. Samir, an
eligible bachelor, loses his choice in the bargain:

> Relatives brought him tempting offers of marriage-
> able daughters of high corporate executives who
> would interest themselves in his career. His mar-
> ried friends suggested their sisters-in-law or cous-
> ins. Finally Samir had to decide between marrying
> a pretty girl and one with the higher dowry. His
> father was overjoyed when he decided the dowry.
>
> (*Candles and Roses* 33)

The dowry plays a significant role in the matrimonial ritual.
The family is guided by considerations of money, prestige
and status rather than the compatibility of the persons who
marry.

Dilip's love for Teresa, an Italian girl, creates a stir in
the familial circle. Bholanath, the head of the family, is
worried about the love marriage. He takes all measures to
keep it a secret. The family pride is at stake:

> He was certain that there was no place for a for-
> eign girl in his family and they were not about to
> give up Dilip. He would think of a way out. He
> still cherished the dream of a union between the
> Mitra family and the Roy Chowdhuris. Now that
> Dilip was qualified and England-returned, it should
> not be too difficult.
>
> (*Portrait on the Roof* 25)

The senior members consider the prestigious connections

more important while the youngsters emphasize their individual likes and dislikes. In such wars within the family
the seniors are generally successful because of their power.
If the juniors are triumphant the family divides and they
are forced to leave their homes to fend for themselves.

The English colonization of India that resulted in mass
education has had its impact on the family system in
India. Aileen D. Ross explicates this process:

> Higher education is more easily obtained in cities,
> and one important outcome of the move to obtain
> it is that children develop ambitions which their
> parents do not share. They also tend to see life in a
> new perspective, and the relative freedom of the
> city makes them reluctant to return to the tutelage
> of the elders.

(*The Hindu Family in its Urban Setting* 25)

Romen Basu chooses these factors for creating the frame-
works for his novels.

The forces which work against the family system and
family life are economic, political and occupational. The
technological forces and industrialisation followed by
urbanisation have slowly brought about the changes in
family patterns. The children leave the parents in search of
employment and consequently they set up nuclear families. Ranjith, Sukumal, Ashoke and Biren leave their parents and families when they acquire jobs in India and
abroad.

However, the security of the family is an illusion and
a dream in the nuclear families. As the larger houses break
into smaller units one can experience the loneliness, especially the young and the old feel neglected in their homes.
On the other hand the social security is the strength of the
joint family because the young and old feel secure. The
sick and the aged are taken care of in the joint families.
The problem of aging proves to be a menace owing to the
increasing nuclear families. Romen Basu in his short story

"A Glass of Water" depicts the dehumanizing life of the aged people in America. In this short story, two ladies Emma and Pearl exchange their old-age experiences. Emma tells how the eastern countries are different in this aspect. The old-age homes are non-existent in the east because the families take care of the old. They compare their own western condition in which the old people are ignored by the younger generation. Pearl's remark arouses pity: "Why do our children feel we are their liability? We cannot change their lives anymore" (*Rustling of Many Winds* 64). They also discuss how the children are unwanted by American parents because the children are considered to be liabilities. Pearl tells Emma about her daughter Ronnie's attitude: "Ronnie says Jeremy was an accident. They didn't want another child. They were looking forward to being free" (66). The western scene is inhuman, and contrasting, when compared to the Indian life pattern. The sympathy for the old and the young is inherent in the Indian culture.

The western culture has often influenced the east. English culture has crept into India along with education. The English people who generally live as nuclear families have been role models for the Indian esoteric. Arun in *A House Full of People* apes the west. He dresses in western fashion, speaks only English and also laughs at Indian customs. He hates everything Indian and tries to draw his cousins to his ways of thinking. Sudhin gauges Arun's behaviour suspecting it to be the western influence, and worriedly tells:

> What is more disturbing, he is influencing his cousins. I hear he tells Bimal, Amal and all the others, how terrible it is to live as one family like this. In Europe as soon as man reaches the age of twenty one, he goes to live on his own. They never live with their parents once they are married. (22)

The boys with education look forward to employment outside seeking freedom in every aspect. The cities where job opportunities are plentiful provide them with an escape from family bondage. The employment takes them away from home and family.

Romen Basu's heroes Ashoke, Sukumal and Biren leave India in search of fortune and freedom. The temptation of the west induces Ashoke to "shake hands with Englishmen and extract orders for bolts, nuts, plywood, anything they were in the market to buy. Three months before graduation I had made enough money to leave for the United Kingdom" (*Your Life to Live* 37). Sukumal leaves India for a different reason. His search for love takes him outside his native land. The forthcoming narration shows how he manages to set foot on a foreign land:

> I enrolled in college, but my plans to get away from home had become an obsession. I was eighteen; the war was over; there was no need for enlisted men, and I had no money to pay for my passage. My only chance was to join the merchant marine as a deck hand.
>
> (*A Gift of Love* 42)

The social, economic and political changes have been destructive to the joint family all over the world. Ralph Linton analyses the breaking of the family:

> Such families broke down under the impact of developing mercantilism with its increase in individual opportunity, while their complete destruction came with the rise of modern mechanized civilization. Here in the United States we have reached the low point in a process of breakdown of kin structure which has reduced our functional kin group to the primary, biologically determined one of parents and children.
>
> ("Cultural and Personality Factors Affecting Economic Growth" 83-84)

The quest for familial harmony is presented in Romen Basu's novels through characters, episodes and dialogue.

Even amidst the disadvantages of the system he sincerely wishes for familial amity. Ranjith perhaps echoes the author's idea when he explains the family security: "We have always felt loved and wanted by every single member of the family. If anything good has come out of our living together, it is a strong sense of security because of the warmth and love given to us" (*A House Full of People* 163). What is absent in the American or western families is the sense of belonging which Basu must have become aware of, thanks to his international experience. So when he infers this truth after his exposure to the world cultures one may argue that his idea is worthy of attention and acclamation.

Romen Basu's progressive ideas about life do not interfere with his love for the so-called old-fashioned idea of living together. One of the characters in *Your Life to Live* honours the system: "It is true that our system is not the best, even though sometimes we argue that it is, at least it is a system which worked for our forefathers and it is working for us" (135). This effective functioning of the system, in addition to its suitability to the Indian culture and life pattern, makes it acceptable to Romen Basu. Hence his plea.

Sukumal who runs away from home to be independent returns to India to overcome his disappointment, in the shelter of the family:

> I like Monuma, Chhotopishima, Se jokakima. I am happy that they are happy. Our cousins have married worthy men — doctors, accountants and engineers. They are all good-natured and obey their wives. No one has any financial worries. My men cousins are all well educated and employed. Everything is fine. I am happy for all that.
>
> (*A Gift of Love* 149)

The consolation which Sukumal cannot get from outside the family drives him home to his family in India. In times of difficulty, the need for the family is human and Sukumal's exodus is nothing strange.

The modern civilization has led to industrialization and urbanisation causing division of homes. The solace of the family is sacrificed for the independence of individuals. Bholanath in *Portrait on the Roof* compares the western society with that of the east glorifying the eastern families:

> Just look at the West. You will find that breaking
> up the family has dehumanized their societies. They
> dread to be old, they resort to all sorts of devices
> to avoid being alone. All scientific values have failed
> so far to replace the comfort of family closeness.
> Why can't we learn from other's mistakes? (7)

Bholanath's words appear to be true to life and thought provoking in the sense that one's knowledge can become another's wisdom.

In the same novel the discussion between Dilip and Arabindo ensures the need for sacrifice by the individual for the family. Dilip is sorry because Arabindo relinquished his love for family integration. Dilip is unable to digest this self-sacrifice because he loves an Italian girl and decides to marry her. Arabindo argues that his renouncing the English girl was essential: "The preservation of the family is rooted in the tradition. To tamper with it is to destroy the system. The ultimate question was how much is it worth to an individual to make a sacrifice to keep the foundation intact" (24). Dilip feels that marriage is an individual choice in which others have no right to interfere. He also feels that a compromise can resolve this problem and says so: "To try to rationalise a forgivable act is hypocrisy. I believe the family would have made the adjustment, even in your time, if you had shown the will to work it out" (24). Romen Basu's love for the preservation of the tradition and his idea as to how it can be modified to suit the modern times are clearly stated without any ambiguity in the form of this dialogue.

Even in Basu's most recent sociological novel, the love for the family is underscored. Onkar Singh's family in *My Own Witness* is an ideal family. Onkar Singh evaluates Avtar's personality: "...thought well of Avtar, a man with feeling for the family. For him, that was the yardstick with which to measure a human being" (87). This can be the highest praise one can pay for the family and Basu pays it consciously and unconsciously.

As a sensitive artist Romen Basu with *minutiae* of details presents the joint family system as prevalent in India. The fact, however, is that the system is slowly dying. As a sensible humanist Basu recommends the joint family system, mainly for its 'values' peculiar to Indian culture. In the days of Sartre, for whom 'Hell is other people' joint family system is perhaps utopian and a myth. As a helpless observer, Basu feels sorry that such a system is degenerating. The system has represented finer elements like love, sentiments, collective responsibility and a sense of sacrifice. The system is having its natural death since Indians are quick to ape anything western.

With a Hegelian perspective — thesis and antithesis — Basu presents the two sides of the joint family system. He makes it quite clear that in the joint family the eldest sons are exploited and they feel exploited, whereas the youngsters feel insignificant and ignored. He does not fail to recognise the fact that youngsters find it difficult to marry either out of caste and religion or out of rank. The inferior state of woman is also made clear though the focus is less emphatic. One can surmise that with all the disparities, the male-chauvinistic attitudes, and the tradition-bound conservative concepts, the joint family system is a unique phenomenon which is quite in keeping with Indian culture and tradition for which the inevitable defects are endured.

Basu who wages a crusade against hierarchy through caste and religion in *Outcast* and *Blackstone* chooses to be tolerant towards similar problems in the novels discussed

in this chapter. The reasons are not far to seek. The para-
dox can be explained through psychological and sociological interpretations. Basu, rooted in Indian tradition and
culture and belonging to a highly traditional West Bengal
family, is fully aware of the rare values the system
provides. All his international experience has only helped
him to confirm the age-old theory that tradition has its
own values against modernity. The researcher was pleas-
antly surprised when Basu went into raptures while discussing joint family system as a phenomenon: "I live in
today's world but I give much more value to yesterday's
world. My values are deeply rooted where my culture is
and from where I draw my sustenance" (Interview). The
fact is that his personal experience in a joint family has
convinced him of these values and that is why he feels the
need for it.

However, when the same injustices are in action at
the social level Basu raises his arms against those iniquities. His battle against the injustice at the societal level is
the concern of the next chapter.

Chapter 3

Societal Discordance

Because stratification issues are so highly charged yet delicately balanced, people often try to sidestep them or deny their importance. They pretend the stratification is natural and desirable whether it is mild or extreme, since even the most equal and open societies in the world contain stratification systems which perpetuate and legitimate some degree of inequality and oppression.

(Richard Cheever Wallace and Wendy Drew
Wallace *Sociology* 248)

India has long been reckoned as having the most stratified society of the world with myriad forms of superordination and subordination. The Indians are deeply involved in moral and ethical questions regarding the caste systems, cultural diversity and economic inequality which form the central issues of social stratification. The coherence and order in a society eventually rest on its stratification.

The stratification implies differentiation among one or more features in such a fashion that they can be grouped along a common axis. In a broader sense, stratification is ranking of social position which influences the social rewards to those in the position. The term includes ranking by caste, class, religion, age, race and office. The societies create social stratification which influences almost all aspects including lifestyle and opportunities.

The status of a person is his/her position in a social structure. This status is determined by various factors — caste, class, religion, occupation, power and sex. Caste is a form of stratification in which an individual is assigned to a particular status based on his/her designation of birth. The fact is that members of the higher castes are much wealthier thereby more powerful than those below in caste. The class stratification ranks the people according to their economic status, which permits mobility between the categories. In a class system, achieved status is determined partly through individual's efforts. A 'caste' is a closed social stratum while class is more open a stratum. However, in typical Indian *milieu* poverty was synonymous until recently with one's low caste status. So, in good many cases the low castes have been lower classes as well. It is manifestly so in Basuli, the main place of action in *Outcast*. Basuli is a typical Indian village, other than being a Bengali village.

Romen Basu is aware of the stratification of Indian society and the evils entailed to it. He looks for harmony in the society as he does in the family. The barriers impeding harmony in the society are the stratification of many factors, especially the caste. The working of stratificational laws is deeply rooted in the minds of the people. So he delves deep into the root causes of stratification. The main reason, as it appears, is the religion. The Indians, especially the Hindus, have blind faith in religion and they accept anything said and done in the name of religion. *The Bhagavad Gita* speaks of the four-fold system of caste as divinely ordained and commands each caste to remain content with performing the duties assigned to it. It commands:

> The four-fold caste system was created by me, by
> differentiating people according to their *guna* and
> *karma*...It is better to follow one's own *dharma* righ-

teously established even with all blemishes, than
the *dharma* of others even when it is more attractive; it is better to die doing one's own *dharma*, the
dharma of others is terrible to follow...So live a righteous life now, do not revolt, accept the lot because
if you are righteous you will have a better deal in
your next life. (IV 13 & III 35)

Saints have interpreted the four-fold caste system in different ways. Swami Chinmayananda interprets the caste system in terms of the *Varna* scheme. He explains:

This is a stanza that has been much misused by the
upholders of the social crime in our recent times
styled as the caste system. *Varna* means different
shades of texture or colour is implied here in the
Yogic sense. In the Yoga Sastra, they attribute some
definite colours to the triple *Gunas*, which means,
as we have said earlier, the mental temperaments.
Thus *Sattva* is considered as white, *Rajas* as red
and *Tamas* as black. Man is essentially the thoughts
that he entertains. From individual to individual
even when the thoughts are superficially the same,
there are clear distinctions contributed by the temperaments in each individual.

(*The Bhagavadgeetha* 397)

In defining *dharma* Swami Chinmayananda argues that
dharma does not simply denote duty but means *Vasanas* i.e.
the texture of thoughts ingrained in the person. According
to him *Swadharma* (one's own dharma) is the predetermined
channel of thinking and taste. When one lives in accordance with his *dharma* the life is one of joy, success and
satisfaction. To act against one's in-born taste and thinking
is *Para-dharma* (dharma of others) which results in disastrous life. Chinmayananda states that these terms have
been misunderstood in the days of Hindu decadence. He
says:

The orthodox group wanting to perpetuate the air-
tight classification of the caste system has tried to

> pull down these two terms into its limited applica-
> tion and have written voluminous commentaries
> upon them which have proved more dangerous to
> our growth than a help to our social and individual
> development.
>
> (*The Bhagavadgeetha* 354)

In the remote past the growth of the caste system was founded on professional specialization and later it became rigid and inflexible. The Brahmins attributed a divine origin to the caste system by following the Rig Veda. V.D. Mahajan corroborates this view: "It (Rig Veda) asserts that the Brahmana was born out of the mouth of Brahma, the Kshatriya from his arms, the Vaishya from his stomach, and the Sudra from his feet. As the Vedas are the revealed books and contain nothing but the truth, the division of society as given therein is attributed to divine ordinance" (*History of India* 87). The institution of caste laid restrictions for the lower classes. The system of elevating and belittling the human beings appeared in the practices of untouch-ability and stratification.

In the *Varna* scheme there is no place for the untouch-able. The untouchables are generally scavengers, sweep-ers, cremators and carriers of waste. The untouchables and chandals are said to be the offspring of a Sudra father and a Brahmin mother. The religious practices concede that the life of the untouchable is one of complete segregation. The untouchable cannot enter all streets and lanes trodden by caste Hindus and they must carry brooms to brush away their polluting footprints. In the southern regions of India the untouchable is prescribed distance, compelling him/ her to keep away from the caste Hindu. The untouchable is expected to shout a warning before entering a street to avoid holier people getting contaminated by his shadow. In some places he could not raise his voice because even the sound of his voice reaching the caste Hindus' ears is deemed to be equally polluting as his touch. They could not enter the Hindu temple and the caste Hindu houses or draw water from the common well. Ghurye exemplifies this degradation of untouchability: "A householder is exhorted to throw some food for them and the outcastes along with that for crows and dogs outside the house, after all the members of the household have taken their meals" (*Caste and Race in India* 79). The abiding caste system has led to the cruel form of untouchability since the lower castes are held in contempt.

The Brahmins who are placed at the apex of the social gradation from time immemorial, try to maintain their superior position. They have held the reins of education and religion which make them significant and powerful in the society. The honour bestowed on the Brahmin community stems from the religious fear and belief which they instilled in the minds of the people. Regarding this position enjoyed by the Brahmins, Vishnu observes:

> The Gods are invisible deities, the Bramins are visible deities. The Bramins sustain the world. It is by the favour of the Bramins that the Gods reside in the heavens; a speech uttered by Bramins (whether a curse or a benediction) never fails to come true. What the Bramins pronounce, when highly pleased if they promise sons, cattle, wealth, or some other boon to a man, the Gods will ratify; when the visible gods are pleased the invisible gods are surely pleased as well.

> (quoted in G.S. Ghurye *Caste and Race in India* 90)

The Brahmins are treated as representatives of God on earth. The Indian society bows its head to the Brahmins willingly without probing into the reasons for their superiority. The lower caste may rise in the echelons of class but still cannot get rid of the hegemony of caste since caste is determined by birth.

The Brahmins are considered to be the authority in

the religious context. The headman occupies the highest position in the secular context. The members of the three higher Varnas—Brahmins, Kshatriyas and Vaishyas—are probably the Aryans, the conquerors. The Sudras, the dark skinned people, are the conquered who are engaged in the services of the three higher varnas. The simple distinction based on occupation between the Vaishyas and Sudras begins to grow into an increasing number of endogamous groups. Social distinctions become more pronounced with the passage of time. It is difficult to trace the origin of the caste system to the exactness of the period.

The social stratification includes a host of factors by which the different castes are separated publicly and demonstrably. The social practices, occupations, lifestyles, rituals and taboos isolate one from the other. This system of exclusions and segregations must have been devised to establish power over the conquered sections. Harold R. Isaacs feels: "It seems likely enough that the purity the Brahmins tried to maintain was not merely ritual and not only political but also racial" (*India's Ex-Untouchables* 31). The superiority they claim is also due to the colour of the skin. They maintained the distance by preaching the 'karma' and the 'dharma' theory. Harold R. Isaacs explicates the 'karma' theory as follows:

> Traditional Hindu doctrine held that they were born to their condition or fate (karma) because of sins committed in an earlier life. If they submitted faithfully and performed their duty (dharma) without complaint in this life, they might not surely, but only might hope for better life the next time around.
>
> (*India's Ex-Untouchables* 32)

The Hindu religion believes that birth is a predestined condition of fate and calls it 'karma'. It also advises that it is the 'dharma' of a person to follow the 'karma' without either questioning or regret. Hence, submission and endurance to any social deterioration becomes possible. The caste prejudices have proved disastrous to the welfare of the society. Rajendra Singh Vatsa holds the view that:

> The system which divides us into innumerable castes claiming to rise by minutely graduated steps from the pariah to the Bramin is a whole tissue of injustice, splitting men into divisions high and low, based not on the natural standard of personal quali- ties but on the accident of birth.

> (*The Depressed Classes of India* ii)

The lower classes are the victims of the caste distinction yet they also refuse to violate the religious customs of the society for fear of God and rebirth. They submit to the onslaughts of the upper classes with the hope that their conditions will improve in the following births.

The caste system of India results in not only inequal- ity but also oppression and exploitation. The major reason why the system is still powerful is that the upper castes finding the system convenient and favourable continue to maintain the caste distinctions. They see to it that the lower castes fight among themselves. The union of lower castes would pose a threat to their superior position. So, the hier- archy within the lower classes is strictly maintained by the upper caste people. In this context, Gerald D. Berreman writes:

> Those low in an [sic] hierarchical system univer- sally see it as disadvantageous to themselves and object either to the system or to the manner in which it is applied to themselves. Any social hierarchy, then, is perpetrated and perpetuated by elites and is struggled against as circumstances permit, by those they oppress.

> ("The Brahmanical View of Caste" 84)

The four-fold division of caste that is lost in millennial obscurity serves as a formative and integrating system, bringing social co-existence and ensuing daily life of inter- dependence. Simultaneously caste is also a medieval tyranny using religious sanctions and preserving fundamental *status quo* and abolishing the personal dignity for the lower castes. William Walsh writes about the influence of religion in India when he traces the growth of Indian English literature:

> In India, religion enfolds body and soul from conception to dissolution. It is the secret premise of family thought and action. It saturates the speech, the hymns, the myths and stories and the idiom of daily life. It exists in forms accessible to the most sophisticated as well as to the least educated, to the austere moralist and the frenzied terrorist.
>
> (*Indian Literature in English* 6)

Walsh's statements expound the Indian *milieu* from where the genre of Indian English literature has originated.

Romen Basu's experiences with the Indian *milieu* have introduced him to the obnoxious practices of caste system. As a rational citizen, he analyses the root cause of this gradation in the society. His support for the downtrodden and the possibilities of achieving a harmonious existence can be seen in his novels. The discordant elements in the family happen to be the social elements which impede the harmony in the society, the effect being malevolent. In trying to achieve the harmony in the society Basu exposes the uncharitable nature of the caste system through mild satire in the earlier novels and with a tinge of sarcasm in his later novels. This change from moderation to vehemence and then to final complacence is indicative of the maturing of the novelist. After his mild response to the gruesome caste system as it affects the family he expands his views to a wider expanse of the society. He moves from the microcosm of the family to the macrocosm of the society. His widening perspective makes him react emotionally towards the social iniquities.

There are glimpses of social satire of caste system in his second novel *Your Life to Live*. Mohan discusses the caste system with his wife Zarina: "Not exactly a social outcaste, after all, our caste system takes care of that. The lower caste Bengalis, for instance, are employed in factories as manual workers and the supervisors and engineers are from a higher caste. The same in the offices, among the clerks you will find few belonging to our caste" (133). How the caste system is maintained forcibly by the seemingly complementary function of different caste appears as a mild statement in this novel.

In *A Gift of Love* Romen Basu attempts to cause social holocaust by uniting the hero Sukumal and the servant's daughter Kajali in marriage. This hypogamous marriage is unusual in Indian families and Basu's attempts to bring about a unity between castes are seen even in his early career. Kajali answers Sukumal smartly: "I am a maid servant; I am not part of society, I never will be. I know you have told me hundreds of times that in Europe, marriage between rich people and maid servants or their class is common. But you are not going to live in Europe" (171). One can see the Indian *milieu* from an international perspective in this statement. The cultural differences between the west and east are distinct.

In the novel *The Tamarind Tree* the tone changes from meek response to severe criticism of the observance of untouchability. The orthodox households adhere to the religious customs tenaciously fearing the wrath of God and religion. The concept of the bodily purity of the upper castes and the practice of the lower castes being treated as pollutants are common in the orthodox households. One such household is presented in this novel where Mohamaya walks on the floor before it is washed, after the sweeper walks in to clean the toilets. When she is ordered to purify her body by a bath she refuses: "I don't believe in untouchables. I grew up with them, shared meals with them" (133). Her defiance is unnerving and she becomes a heretic in their eyes. *Mejokakima* forbids her to enter her room without changing her dress. The women who happen to brush against her run to bathe to get rid of the pollution. The religious customs recommend various amends for the violation of the laws of religion by way of atonement. Rajendra Singh Vatsa records the pardons in the religious scripts: "...the expiation for which is a bath, the shaving of the face or the handing over a substantial fine to the Brahmins" (*The Depressed Classes of India* 3). Romen Basu who has a comprehensive knowledge about the religious observance, pictures the senior members as orthodox and superstitious. The youngsters like Mohamaya represent modernity and social protest.

Romen Basu's interest in social affairs increases gradually with his writing career as seen in the novels. In *The Tamarind Tree* he pictures an incident in which a Muslim is forbidden to enter the house because Muslims are generally lower caste converts. The food brought by the Muslim is ordered to be thrown out by the lady of the house. Anukul demands an explanation for this act because he knows for sure that the food is prepared in a Hindu hotel. She rebukes him: "Don't talk nonsense. A muslim servant carried them here. Besides, do you have to believe whatever he said" (140)? The ladies are staunch observers of the religious customs and they cannot brook any violation of these rules. The segregation in this event is caste and not religion. The Muslims and the Christians assume themselves to have been extricated from caste. But the fact remains that untouchability exists everywhere. Harold R. Isaacs writes his experiences regarding conversion:

> The Harijan Christians in some regions were kept outside the Church. Then they were allowed to sit in the Church in a separate wing. Even today Christians belonging to untouchable castes are forced to have separate cemeteries in some parts of India. Even the dead must observe caste and untouchability...Muslims have told me that they generally do not tolerate marriages between higher caste

Muslims and the scavenging Muslims or butcher Muslims...

(India's Ex-Untouchables 171)

The roots of the caste system run very deep and Romen Basu believes that the caste system cannot be eradicated as long as blind faith in religions exists in people.

Outcast is a thoroughly sociological novel after the phase of the family-based novels. This novel deals with the injustices meted out to the lower castes. Sambal, a chandal, suffers abject humiliation in the hands of the zamindar. The zamindar treats Sambal's father as a worm. The untouchable is accused of entering the Kali temple and the zamindar shouts at him: "If God cared for you, how could you be born a chandal, untouchable who burns dead bodies, you son-of-a-bitch" (2). The temple entry is an unpardonable sin according to the zamindar. Even the neighbours of Mahanta who belong to the lower caste blame him for his unholy act. They question him, "What came over him to enter a place so sacred, when even the worst criminals have resisted the temptation" (5)? The police inspector who is supposed to implement the governmental law reproaches Mahanta instead of supporting him. The inspector accuses him, "That's obvious, you son-of-a-pig. Had you no fear of punishment for walking up those holy steps, where you and your kind are debarred" (1)? Temple entry of an untouchable is not encouraged by any section of the society for religious reasons. They think that the defilement of Gods is an irredeemable sin. The zamindar is unable to digest the idea of an untouchable stepping into the temple. He says, "I cannot believe what I hear, that untouchable entered our temple and polluted our Kalima. What curse will we have to bear for this" (4)? Romen Basu pivots the story on the temple entry of Mahanta, an untouchable and presents the response of the general public. He highlights the social injustice by capturing the Indian ethos in this novel.

According to law, the untouchables are allowed to enter any temple. They can use public wells and can have access to shops and restaurants, without discrimination. Penalties are not only levied on those who obstruct the exercise of these rights but on those who abuse untouch-ability. However, every untouchable experiences the discrimination in traditional forms or new shapes both in village and in city. There have been changes but an un-touchable is reminded of his status or lack of it. Harold R. Isaacs rightly remarks in this regard: "The waving of these legal wands obviously did not cause untouchability to dis-appear" (*India's Ex-Untouchables* 48). Romen Basu is con-scious of the unlawful discrimination. His themes centre around these burning issues and the reader's response is sought to be produced. The conversation between two char-acters in *Outcast* reveals the basis for social stratification:

> "...Don't the lower castes have the right by law to enter any temple, anywhere?"
>
> "To hell with the law. We don't allow such a God defying law to be practised here."
>
> "There are two kinds of law, one made by man and the other by God. We are willing to obey the law that does not go against God's will." (16)

The fear of God and religion controls the mind and day-to-day activities of the people. They are blind to the human values and the injustice is done with the express sanction of religion. Basu depicts the injustices inflicted on the lower classes quite tellingly. The village of Basuli in *Outcast* is a place where "Not only were men and women of the lower castes barred from entering the temple courtyard, but even their animals were badly beaten if one strayed in by chance" (11). This explains the deep-rootedness of the caste system. It does not result from inequality but from oppression and exploitation of the low castes by the higher castes.

Sambal, the hero of *Outcast*, unlike the other chandals

understands that the exploiters cannot be wiped out as long as the exploited people allow themselves to be exploited. He is courageous enough to oppose the injustice. In his conversation with *mastermoshai* he discloses his heart: "I tell them that if Sudras could find a place among Bramins and Kayasthas, so could we once they are convinced that God did not make them untouchables, they will be ready to fight" (40). Sambal analyses the real cause of the social problem. He feels that religion prevents man from fighting for his basic rights. The pathetic condition, as it appears, is that even the lower castes believe in the caste system as intensely as their higher caste counterparts. Dubois explains that pitiable predicament when he talks about the pariyans, a lower class in South India:

> The idea that he was born to be in subjection to the other castes is so ingrained in his mind that it never occurs to the Pariah to think that his fate is anything but irrevocable...Nothing will ever persuade him that men are all made of the same clay.
>
> (quoted in Michael Moffatt *An Untouchable Community in South India: Structure and Consensus* 7)

The lower classes in India accept subjugation without questioning and regret.

Romen Basu's response to the social problems results in works of art. In the novel *Blackstone* one can find his response tinged with emotion and anger unlike *Outcast* in which the reaction is only passive. Sambal in *Outcast* and Kalapathor in *Blackstone* lose their fathers because of the tyranny of the higher caste people but they react differently. Sambal could only say to the zamindar: "You are meddling in the affairs of the lower castes because you smell profit. You will do anything to corrupt these ignoramuses" (*Outcast* 200). Sambal's reaction is milder when compared to that of Kalapathor who reprimands before taking away the life of the zamindar, "Shut up, damn you. Your days are finished. My father was a victim of your tyranny. Many have died of hunger and from your cruelty. You will die the same way you took the lives of others" (*Blackstone* 15). Romen Basu's response shows a shift from meekness to defiance and retaliation. This not only underscores the historical events which happened during Naxalite movement, but also explains the psychological factors behind such incidents. Ravindranathan corroborates this view when he makes a comparative study of the two novels: "What has begun as a desperate, yet humble appeal in *Outcaste* [sic], takes a violent turn in *Blackstone*, since by now political awareness has become a possibility" ("Quest for Justice: A reading of Romen Basu's *Outcast* and *Blackstone*" 8).

As the social scene changes from *Outcast* to *Blackstone* one can find a change in the social atmosphere. The people who succumb to humiliation and despotism in *Outcast* either attempt to revolt or show their protest against the social injustice in *Blackstone*. The women in *Outcast* are weak and passive. Biresh's wife needs two ounces of mustard oil. She goes to a nearby brahmin grocery store to avoid walking two miles. She covers her head to conceal her identity. The shopkeeper discovers her caste by the way she wears *sindur*. When she begs for oil he pours the oil from his high seat, spilling half of it on the ground. She demands for more oil as a compensation for the spilt oil and the shopkeeper carelessly rebukes: "Shut up, you damn woman. Scoop it off the ground" (*Outcast* 48). The untouchables are not treated as equal with other men anywhere, be it the temple or the shop. The untouchables do not realise the exploitation and accept it as their fate and 'karma'. In *Blackstone* the women are shown to be more aggressive and demanding. Karuna, a peasant woman of a lower caste, addresses a group of other chandal women:

> Until recently, peasant women have been trampled on as worms. Rich women can afford the luxury of sitting in chairs, getting their feet massaged and drinking tea, cup after cup. But poor women like

us have always helped their husbands, fathers and
brothers in the fields and factories. (41)

The attitude of the lower castes appears to have a different
tide from submission to aggression as one reads through
the two novels.

The lower castes allow themselves to be exploited and
endure oppression because they too believe in the religion
which degrades them. A farmer in *Outcast* tells:

> I am a lower caste too. I know what our society
> expects from us and I respect it. If my master takes
> sixty percent of the share of the crop, doing noth-
> ing while I sweat blood to grow food on his arid
> land what can I do? I accept it. (8)

On the other hand, the villagers of *Blackstone* resist the
tyranny of the exploiters unlike the villagers of Basuli in
Outcast. The villagers gather outside the police station to
cry out their grievances:

> What do you want to print? Come with us, we'll
> take you to Gour Haldar's house. The haramzada's
> family robbed us of our lives, paying us starvation
> wages. He lent us money at five hundred percent,
> he raped our women, he thrashed our men. What
> has the God-damn government ever done for us?
> Now we will take the land by force. We are ready
> for war, we are ready to die, we will kill the jothdars
> to the last man and the police, and all the
> other enemies of society. Print anything you want.
> If you say anything false, better not return to this
> village again. (18)

The tone, language and the matter bear resistance and violence in the latter novel. The forbearance in the previous
novel has turned to protest as if that can serve as the answer to the problem. One may infer that the author wants
to suggest a solution to the problem of caste-based suppression in the name of ferocity. Violence, in the process, is
inevitable. History has only confirmed the concept. Con-

sider for example the Naxalite movement of Bengal or the Agrarian revolution of Tanjore.

Social changes are not brought about overnight. The individuals who oppose the existing condition seek the support of organizations to carry out their plans. Sambal and Kalapathor come across identical situations. As they fall a prey to the despotic zamindars, they join the communist party to wipe away the class and caste discriminations. Sambal tries to gather people for support. When his plans fail, he joins the communist party. His steps are guarded when he says:

> My point is no one can depend upon the promises of the Brahmins and Kayasthas. They may say one thing to us and something else to the Bagdis. You have to give me an assurance that if soft soaping does not work, we will use force. I want the temple management changed first, but that is not all. You have to agree to go beyond that and insist on a plan of social intercourse, even marriage between the lower castes. Are you prepared to do that?

> (*Outcast* 237)

Sambal is not unaware of the political mechanisms and party gimmicks. Shakuntala Narasimhan aptly remarks:

> The confrontation between the outcast and the *zamindar* takes on political overtones when the communists and the Congress party vie with each other to bring "progress" to the village by promoting one or the other faction according to what would serve their political ends best. And in these manoeuvrings, Sambal, whose idealism sees only black or white and no shades in between, is a misfit.

> ("Shadows in the countryside" *Indian Express* 20)

Sambal becomes a misfit because he is not prepared for a compromise. However, he wants to achieve his target. The absence of mass support from the people weakens his attempts.

Sambal uses all persuasive methods whilst Kala-pathor's instantaneous step is fierce: "With a wicked blow from his axe, he sliced off Gour's right shoulder. As Haldar lay bleeding and unconscious, Kalapathor went berserk, hacking and striking and trampling on Haldar before he finally struck off head" (*Blackstone* 16). Kalapathor seems to believe that terroristic activities would pay good divi-dends. Basu has had a thorough personal knowledge of the Naxalite movement and what he presents is only a 'slice of life'. This does not, perhaps, mean that he either recommends or justifies violence.

Romen Basu creates a social awareness by his pictur-esque events. In *Outcast* the temple has been the hotbed of trouble. Mahanta, Sambal's father, undergoes undue suf-ferings in the hands of the zamindar for entering the Kali temple. Again, the people of Basuli witness a demonstra-tion of an outburst during the inauguration of a temple exclusively for the untouchables. In the last scene, Sambal decides to blow up the temple. He says, "Once the temple is reduced to rubble, all the lower castes will understand what I am protesting about intensely" (*Outcast* 244). The temple appears as a myth and witness to all the injustices done on its behalf. By making the temple the central issue the author drives home the idea that God is helpless and religion is behind the brutalities.

The characters Kesab and Kalapathor believe that un-daunted courage can intimidate the upper class. Kesab discusses ways and means to strengthen his party:

> The most important thing is to instil in the mind of landowners that they will have to live in fear. Take the head of the most cruel jothdar first. Whatever is collected from his grain stor-age, use it to feed the starving. The attacks should be organized one by one. If you follow this policy, you won't need many arms. (9)

The policy of Sambal in *Outcast* is exhortation while the path of Kesab is detonation. Kesab plans to wipe away the upper class in toto. This Machiavellian sense of believing that 'Might is Right' underscores the fact that by now the suppressed people have become desperate.

The caste system has a vertical order and the differences between castes are felt at every level. Haripada and Mahanta are both members of the lower castes. Haripada belongs to a slightly superior caste to that of Mahanta. When Mahanta's wife suffers labour pains, Haripada refuses help in the name of the caste. He scoffs at him: "My caste is superior to yours. We go to the same tea shop, but that's as far as it goes" (*Outcast* 10), to which Mahanta replies rudely: "You collect animal hides and I work with dead human bodies, yet you place yourself above me. You are sick" (10-11). What is beyond rational understanding is that feuds are common amongst lower classes. One clan holds the next lower one in contempt. Man is not only divided by power or physical prowess but by caste hierarchy which is decided even at birth. Romen Basu is sensitive to these evils of hierarchy. The lower castes besides being unmindful of the exploitation by the upper castes are at the same time divided among themselves. The religious bearing bars man from thinking for himself. They resign to their lot with equanimity. The Indian veneration of rituals and ritualists gets revealed in the following narration: "He (The priest) had had to borrow the raw silk dhoti and wrapper because it was important for him to let everyone understand that a priest of a temple for the untouchables was no less important than other priests" (*Outcast* 197). The untouchables also engage a brahmin priest for their temple not realizing that their reverence to their higher caste leads to degradation of their own caste.

Romen Basu shows another instance in *Blackstone* which endorses the fealty of the lower caste to the upper caste. Kalapathor a chandal and a communist reveres the party leader Kesab. The respect arises out of caste superiority. Kalapathor who vouchsafes to wipe away the zamindars still feels the discrimination of caste. He says

about Kesab: "Comrades or not, I can never forget that he
is a bramin and I am santhal. Besides, his intellect scares
me — he can always convince me with his logic, even
when my heart tells me he is wrong" (*Blackstone* 150). This
instance proves that the caste system, which is very much
deep-rooted, is difficult to be eradicated.

As one reads through the novels of Romen Basu, the
social and political climate appears to have changed for the
better. The condition of the lower castes in *Outcast* is worse
when compared to that of *Blackstone*. The public does not
support the cause of the untouchables. Girija suffers im-
mensely because he supports the cause of Sambal. His family too is victimized and the zamindar seizes every oppor-
tunity to pressurize him to pay the debts knowing his
inability to pay:

> His *naib* came twice that week, demanding that
> Girija pay up for two of his three acres or within a
> week, the court would auction whatever he pos-
> sessed. That meant the pair of bullocks and the
> plough. The zamindar was determined to evict from
> his land every peasant who was disloyal to him.
>
> (*Outcast* 44)

Girija's son is sent home with a bloody nose and a warning not to return to school. Sambal's associates suffer
mortification. Saraju, a widow, forbids Sambal to visit her
convincing him with reasons:

> No, No. Please don't come here again. If they see
> you in front of my house, I will be hauled up again
> before the Gram Panchayat. *Since I am a widow, the*
> *question of justice does not arise,* I learned that today.
> (124) (Emphasis added)

Sambal's acquaintances are forced to suffer with him. The
passing reference of the predicament of widows is a point
to ponder. The Feminist in Romen Basu — Basu claims
that he is writing a Feminist novel at present and the above
passage proves his sensitivity to feministic issues.

The author hopes for a bright future devoid of the evils of the present society. He not only aims at it but endeavours to bring about a social change by creating the social awareness in the minds of the readers. The hope for better prospects can be inferred from the author's presentation.

In *Blackstone* even educated boys and girls participate in party activities in favour of the lower castes. Rontu the son of an officer tells his mother that he is joining fifty other students to partake in an outbreak of violence:

> I have chosen to serve the poor, the desperately neglected, those who have no hopes, those who need a chance to live. I will probably die with a bomb exploding in my hands, but I must try to help others. Your love has given me the courage to help other mothers make their sons and daughters strong. (27)

This public support for the cause of the downtrodden is not to be seen in the previous novel *Outcast*. The women also take up arms: "Malati's husband, a front-line fighter, has already trained his wife to work with him from the time he joined the rebels. She had been with her husband when he made plastic bombs and when he stabbed a policeman" (*Blackstone* 41). When the two novels are compared what appears suggestive in *Outcast* is seen carried out in *Blackstone*. The historical fact that any suppression will lead to a revolution has been emphasized here.

The need for education is an important factor that obstructs the road to equality. Basu's novels are emphatic of this fact. Putki, a rational character in the novel, feels that the condition of the lower castes and classes cannot improve until they smell education. She tells Sambal: "When we can read the law, and not be told about it, that will be the day we may speak of justice. Until then our peace lies in accepting we are different and will be treated differently under the law" (*Outcast* 27). Other than picturing the existing condition Basu's novels analyse the situation thoroughly.

In *Blackstone* Kalapathor feels the same way as Putki feels in *Outcast*. He tells Sabitri, "My world was not different from yours, but I have to learn something new every day. Some say that revolution is according to the path followed by China, others disagree. Wish I could read, then perhaps I could judge for myself who is right" (*Blackstone* 101). Education, as eye opener, is denied to the lower castes in order to prevent them from reasoning, questioning and opposing.

Romen Basu emphasises the significance of education in the development of the society in *The Street Corner Boys*:

> There are no aristocrats left in Bengal. Those who had the opportunity, left for England, USA and minor families left for Delhi, Punjab or wherever. Bengali culture has provided us with the sustenance to embrace Marxism. Even the rural poor are 'intellectual', if they have the choice between buying a book, or flash light, they will go for the book. Our folk culture and this habit of reading made us more open than other parts of India. (145)

Romen Basu unambiguously states that education can pave the way for a classless and casteless society.

Basu by narrating innumerable instances of caste superiority in *Outcast* drives home the point that segregating the lower caste is unjust. The onus of inhuman activities lies with the caste sentiments. Romen Basu comprehends a society free from these cold-blooded activities resulting from caste discrimination. In his search for harmony he juxtaposes the ill-natured caste distinction with a world of perfection. The crudities, thus, indirectly lay the foundation for a harmonious living. In *Outcast* Shefali relates the pathetic story of a lower caste man who is bitten by a cobra meets with death because the villagers refuse to carry him and the doctor available is not prepared to treat him free of cost. By the time he is taken to a snake charmer life passes out. Putki after hearing this brutal behaviour of the villagers solemnly tells: "I hear even a Brahmin will drink water offered by a snake charmer to save his life. A barber can enter their temple to perform rituals, although not to pray, all to serve a purpose and our castes are still so unbending" (137).

Putki's social acumen is obvious in her activities. Towards the end of the novel, she drowns herself when Sambal rejects her and the hope for prospective future draws to an end. Romen Basu weaves a different plot with the same characters in the short story "Sambal and Putki". In the short story, the Gram Panchayat fixes exorbitant dowry for the marriage: "Supporters of Kanai argued that Putki was not worth the bother without a set of silver plates, a milk giving cow, cash for a fish pond and a wrist watch for Sambal" (*Rustling of Many Winds* 44). Putki ends her life, in the short story for want of dowry. Putki's death in the novel is caused by caste discrimination while class is behind her end in the short story. The tragedy as depicted in the story is not a simple love tragedy. It deals with human life in a particular situation where everyone has a share in the sorrow, born out of a social system having distorted values. Veena Singh's review in the *Indian Book Chronicle* underscores the stark reality of the caste system in the novel:

> The incidents related by Basu may seem exaggerated to the urban elite, but the fact remains that untouchability is still practised in many parts of the country. Basu has done well to highlight this sordid aspect of Indian society. His characters may not be real, but their harassment and misery are definitely true to life. (151)

Romen Basu is aware of the impediments in the form of caste and class; he knits a tragic story underlining their ill effects.

The people of *Outcast* are afraid of the upper castes because of their faith in religion. Romen Basu characterizes

Sambal in such a way that it creates an awareness in the minds of the readers. Sambal, though uneducated, thinks rationally. His disappointment with the society is revealed when he says:

> I am utterly discouraged...I cannot accept that the upper castes will go on with their high-handed ways for another hundred years. If the lower castes are allowed to remain divided, don't delude yourself that progress will come in spite of it. (142)

Sambal appears to voice Basu's opinion that unity among the lower castes is a condition, requisite to resist the dominant upper caste people. The suggestion for a positive change is made and the possibility of a better future is indicated and visualized.

The Chairman of the party is stubborn in his views that only a revolution can bring about a change. He decries, "I don't like to remind any one of you here that if a nation of seven hundred million people is not willing to sacrifice a few lives, why are we calling it a revolution? No, I will not accept that" (*Blackstone* 74). The Chairman is convinced that the people must join hands to rise against the unfair dealings of the zamindars. The party members are successful in carrying out the expectations of the Chairman. They win the public support to the party demonstrations. This indiscriminate activity, though terroristic, is motivated by a quest for a harmonious living. The faith in the revolution for a good cause mirrors Romen Basu's attitude to life.

The peasants along with the students get involved in the party activities. They do not fear the upper class. Neither do they fear their own class. Revolution is in their veins. The peasants draw inspiration from Kalapathor whose heart is hardened. Kalapathor's love for Sabitri does not alter his revolutionary spirit. He tells her: "My life will never change. I shall die a revolutionary, even if there is no party, no leader. My sister's death will always remind

me that there are too many helpless people who need pro-
tection" (*Blackstone* 101-102). The characters in *Blackstone*
opt for an immediate response. They do not believe in a
gradual change or methods of persuasion adopted by the
people of *Outcast*. Kesab, Kalapathor, Mukul and the tribal
leader join together to form a party of their own. This
occasion warrants an emotional speech. Kesab makes a
fiery speech:

> We must have a plan ready for them first. They
> will be our army of revolutionary thoughts. We
> shall send them to every hut in the district. They
> will tell every individual member that we are not
> surrendering. In our revolutionary struggle, there
> is no point of return. The days of fighting are not
> over, we will not relent until we become the
> masters of the nation's destiny. (160)

The seeds of the revolution are sowed in *Outcast* and they
sprout into blooms and foliages in *Blackstone*.

Romen Basu presents a conducive atmosphere for the
lower castes in the next novel *The Street Corner Boys*. The
condition of the downtrodden has improved with the passage of time and Basu accepts it as a favourable change.
The fury in the previous novel calms down with an understanding of the human mind. In *The Street Corner Boys*,
Ghonu a Ghosh lane boy is appointed the minister of social and humanitarian affairs. The higher-ups show interest in the welfare of the poor. Kesab, the son of a barrister
with a post-graduate degree, is a full-time party worker.
Tarun, the grandson of a retired judge, devotes his services to the party work. Pradipta, member of the royal
family, is a full-time worker of the leftist organization. The
dream of Basu — different castes, classes coming to live
together in unison — the visualisation of an elevation is
thus presented.

The party workers exhibit a different trend in *The Street
Corner Boys*. In the earlier novels the party people indulge
in violence to fight for their rights. They conduct strikes to

show their protest. They are prepared to sacrifice their lives, if necessary. Unlike in these novels, in *The Street Corner Boys* the party workers are engaged in constructive work, for improving the living conditions of the poor people. Basu describes a slum: "The new generation in the *bustis* earned power in their own right. They were all smiles during the day and mighty strong at night. The politics of Calcutta helped to elevate their income higher than that of any other class" (137). This is quite in contrast to the pathetic condition of the poor people in *Outcast* where starvation and poverty have taken their toll.

The political background of *The Street Corner Boys* is freedom struggle. It should be pointed out that this novel deals with a period much earlier than the one depicted in *Outcast*. The social conditions in the period, portrayed in *The Street Corner Boys*, should have been worse. Yet, in this novel the author does not advocate, openly or otherwise, a head-on collision between the oppressors and oppressed. It is not that he is condoning injustice. He shows a gradual and evolutionary approach in the matter of bringing about social harmony. The Gandhian ideals are popular and the people believe in non-violence. Essentially terrorism and terrorist activities are not encouraged. The need for protest and violence has considerably reduced. Romila explains the political canvas:

> The Forward Block's policies are based on Subhas Bose's own ideas. He will take away the national leadership role from other parties all over India by his dedicated struggle. No terrorism, no wheel spinning, his party will have an armed wing with military trained men and women. The party will declare war against the British for national liberation. (69)

What is significant on the part of the writer is that his understanding of the world is undergoing a maturing process.

The status of women in *Outcast* is worse when compared to the later novels. The orthodox society of *Outcast*
lays more restrictions upon women. Saraju Bala Dasi, a
widow, is summoned before the *Gram Panchayat* to answer
the charges of immorality. She is ordered to cover her head
as is expected of her while appearing before men. The
President of the Panchayat says:

> Other women in the room have their heads cov-
> ered. Don't you have any sense of shame as a
> widow to dress the way you do? Do you know of
> another woman in your situation in any of the
> twenty surrounding villages, who makes herself
> pretty for someone else's husband? (121)

She is punished without proper trial, and a penalty of ten
rupees is levied and she refuses to pay. The miserable
plight of the widows in the Indian society by way of social
customs is delineated as one of the many injustices inflicted on womenfolk. Sambal defies the orders of the
Panchayat by meeting Saraju and instigates her to break
the orders of confinement to her place. He says with con-
viction: "Some women are jealous of your independence,
but many wives would like to have your freedom. You can
help other women to understand that they must not subject themselves to tyranny" (*Outcast* 124). The author shows
Saraju as a model woman who lives independently and
does not care about the remarks. He lays the foundation
for feministic views by making his women characters bold
and unconventional.

Ganga's story in *Outcast* is pathetic. She walks to a
nearby village to consult a Muslim doctor. Once when she
goes to get medicines, there is delay and so the Muslim
doctor gives her some food which she accepts. On her
return, her husband demands explanations for her delay.
When he comes to know that she has taken food in the
house of a Muslim, he locks her in the house with her
child and sets fire to it. The neighbours, instead of saving

her life, argue whether sharing a meal with a Muslim is right or wrong. Finally, in order to save the culprit, they agree to report to the police that it is an accidental fire. These instances are examples of caste discrimination and gender inequality. Romen Basu through such vignettes exposes the fact that people turn anti-human as a result of the rampant caste prejudices. Their adherence to certain life-cherished beliefs blinds them to the values of humanism.

The equality of sexes can best be a dream at most times, yet Sambal and Putki discuss the possibilities of women participating in party work. The existing condition is not suitable to practise feministic ideals yet Sambal thinks ahead. He talks about the possible way through which women can help the movement: "You will be a good go-between. Everybody likes you, you can carry messages for us. You don't realise how important that work is. If messages did not get across to the right people, at the right time, we could have explosions. I don't mean just bomb explosions" (*Outcast* 114).

In *Blackstone*, the women enjoy a better position. Sabitri joins party work, sharpens spears, carries messages to the other commander and considers herself a rebel. She tells Kalapathor: "If men treat us as their inferiors, they will not find what they are looking for. Reward will come to those who know how to give" (40). The women nurse the wounded and attend to miscellaneous tasks. Karuna, a party worker, pleads with a crowd of womenfolk to join the protests. She instils a spirit of independence in them by her thought-inspiring speech: "Our leader has made it clear that there is only one class and one caste among comrades. These women will share our beds, our food and our responsibility equally" (42). There is a sign of growth towards modernity in the women characters. Such a presentation foresees a bright promising future for women.

In the later novel *The Street Corner Boys* the modernity of women is baffling. Romila, a college girl, argues for her college education. She is quite different from the Indian orthodox women. Basu presents her as an enterprising woman who is least bothered about detracting comments: "Most of the things she liked were unorthodox. She was fond of watching football matches, playing cricket with younger cousins and occasionally appearing among the street corner boys, even though unwelcome" (40). Romen Basu lays the foundation for feministic trends promoting gender equality. His interest in writing for the cause of women may be attributed to his awareness that women suffer inferior position in India. Especially in the Hindu societies the women are kept subdued. As a committed feminist Basu takes up the cause of women because he sincerely feels that they are deliberately overridden. His interview confirms him to be a feminist:

> This is the biggest, most common 'cause' in my next novel. I feel women are the most discrimi-nated, most underprivileged. The men do not give their women the slightest chance. (Interview)

Basu's women try to struggle their way out of the customs and taboos serving as model women.

Romen Basu moves to a higher plane dealing with racial injustice and discrimination in his later novel *My Own Witness*. This novel shows the problem of Sikhs in the light of politics. The cause of the minority is a universal problem which forms the theme of the novel. The Sikhs who have been victimized both by the Hindus and the Muslims resort to violence and terrorist activities. Sambal in *Outcast* resists the caste superiority. Kalapathor annihi-lates the zamindars by way of wreaking vengeance. Onkar Singh, the hero of *My Own Witness*, shows forbearance even after seeing the damages done to the Golden Temple by the Indian army. He also investigates the cause behind the bureaucracy of the desecration of the Golden Temple. In his search for the reasons behind the cruelty, he be-comes a mystic searching for truth. The quest for truth ushers in the quest for harmony. Onkar Singh is an embodiment of erudite scholarship, religious tolerance and martyrdom. Onkar Singh does not acquiesce in the sacrilege committed by the army in the holiest of Sikh shrine. Yet, he does not resort to violent retaliation. Instead, he begins on a course of contemplation and seeks a universal solution for harmony. Onkar Singh does not react like Sambal nor does he show fits of passion like Kalapathor. His complacent nature symbolizes endurance and universal brotherhood. Onkar Singh propagates universal religion:

> From the little that I have learned from the *Bhagavad Gita* and the *Holy Koran*, they offer the same message as Guru Granth Sahib. Violence, attachment, avarice and wrath, these are four rivers of fire; whoever follows them is consumed. Only those who have God's grace swim across.

> (*My Own Witness* 229)

A reference to Bernard Shaw's "The Devil's Disciple" at this juncture owing to the semblance to the character of Onkar Singh—Richard Dudgeon like Onkar Singh accepts death in the place of Anderson. His motiveless sacrifice takes him high above other characters. He tells Judith, Anderson's wife, prior to his death sentence:

> What I did last night, I did in cold blood caring not half so much for your husband, or [ruthlessly] for you [she droops, stricken] as I do for myself. I had no motive and no interest: all I can tell you is that when it came to the point whether I would take my neck out of the noose and put another man's into it, I could not do it. I don't know why not: ...I should have done the same for any other man in the town, or any other man's wife. (239)

The need for integrity is seen in both the characters. They perpetuate by standing the test of time.

In a secular country like India Romen Basu discerns the need for religious tolerance and characterises Onkar

Singh accordingly. His desire for universal oneness and harmony is manifested in the novel. The give and take policy which he advocates for harmony in the family, is seen extended to the society also. Or in other words, Basu pursues his quest for harmony in his writing. Whatever the stage and actors may be, the author is guided by his commitment to harmony.

The Sikh consciousness has been dealt with by writers like Khushwant Singh. When a non-Sikh, Basu, writes with equal commitment, it is worthy of praise. Onkar Singh, during his confinement to the cell, reads world scriptures. The exposure to the religious truths widens his perspective. His handwritten statement that is read in the court bears testimony to his introspection and meditation: "What the Golden Temple symbolises for me is the same as for people of different faiths for their sacred places of worship. Non-Sikhs do not hate our Guru, so why should they hate our gurudwaras? They do not" (*My Own Witness* 235). The realisation of truth with a genuine understanding of human sympathies is thus brought out.

The author reaches universal heights when he portrays the problem of Sikhs, a minority community in India. When he writes, "Their (Sikhs) plight is a microcosm of all the injustices against minorities throughout the world" (*My Own Witness* 236), the religious sentiments of the Sikhs are respected. This problem of the minority has been experienced by several sections of people for different reasons from time immemorial. When Romen Basu draws the attention of the readers to the Sikh problem, he universalises their cause — the 'cause' of the minorities — the 'cause' of the downtrodden.

As a mature artist Romen Basu is able to bring out the subtle difference between act and attitude. In his earlier novels which mainly centre around family life, the cause of women and injustice of lower caste are not much discussed. The older generation in the fictional world of Basu glues to the traditional rules which the younger generation rebels against. With all the artistic objectivity one can identify the smypathies of Basu for the younger generation. But he does not bring the older generation under scorching sarcasm because it is a question of values. If at all there is any class/caste consciousness in the joint family it is natural and uninhibited. The values are to be cherished and for the sake of such values Basu is prepared to condone the defects.

On the other hand, in the later novels one finds disharmony resulting from caste/class consciousness in the society. The attitude of the higher caste people is consciously bitter and ego-based. The suppressed caste also becomes gradually sensitive to the insult and attempts to fight it out. The stratification becomes social injustice which is the concern of this chapter. From the sensitive and brutal Sambal to the philosophically tolerant Onkar Singh, there is a consistent and gradual growth on the part of the writer. The response to the crises he witnesses in the society undergoes a change which indicates a wiser and more mature artist emerging. How artistically and effectively the archetypal social theme of injustice has been brought out in the novels of Romen Basu is the concern of the next chapter.

Chapter 4

Art as Technique

> *Truly art is a sort of subterfuge. But thank God for it,*
> *we can see through the subterfuge if we choose. Art has*
> *two great functions. First it provides an emotional expe-*
> *rience. And then, if we have the courage of our own*
> *feelings, it becomes a mine of practical truth. We have*
> *had the feelings ad nauseam. But we've never dared dig*
> *the actual truth out of them, the truth that concerns us,*
> *whether it concerns our grandchildren or not.*

(D.H. Lawrence "The Spirit of Place" 123)

An artist is necessarily a man first and he maintains a delicate balance among his private self, professional self and the society. When the balance tilts in favour of any one of these aspects it decides the author's motive, if there is any. It is difficult to assess the artistic values of Romen Basu, he being a living writer.

Romen Basu may be taken to be a Marxian writer on account of his Bengali background, and some of the views found expressed in his works. Again, his observation of Marxian ideas is likely to deceive one into believing that Basu is a Marxian writer. When one looks through the propagandistic views, they provide one stratum of meaning but his works lend themselves to many strata of meanings as great works of art should. The fact remains that he eludes all the characteristics of Marxian writers and emerges as an artist.

Romen Basu's novels may be viewed in the light of Lenin's idea of literature:

> Literature in his [Lenin's] view fulfils a social function; it serves as a guide for revolutionary action by arousing, maintaining and enhancing people's awareness of social realities, and it profits in the turn from the lessons taught by revolutionary struggle. Viewed in this light Marxist esthetics becomes a sort of technology of indoctrination and propaganda; its purpose is to discover how art and literature can be used to control and shape political attitude.

> (Henri Arvon *Marxist Esthetics* 14-15)

Romen Basu's novels do not seem to fulfil the demands of Marxian literature. He arouses the reader into revolutionary thinking but his purpose is not to make the reader a revolutionary. No doubt, the readers are aware of the social realities such as untouchability and the evils of the caste system but he does not use literature as a 'weapon' to instil political ideas in his readers.

Raymond Williams makes a distinction between the 'social' novel and 'personal' novel. He subdivides the 'social' novel into descriptive social novels and documentaries which present a particular working community. The function of this novel lies in shaping the minds of the readers. There is a lively pattern of a materialization of a formula society. *Brave New World, Nineteen Eighty Four* and nearly all science fictions come under this category. In this kind of novel, society is not just a background, but almost a participant. The day-to-day life does not appear even in partial guise playing the role of a character. It is altogether a new world about which Raymond Williams says: "Society is outside the people, though at times, even violently, it breaks in on them" ("Realism and the contemporary novel" 587). Romen Basu's society is neither a formula society nor a documentary society. It is not limited to one section of a society either. Basu's society is life-like.

The aristocracy, the proletariat and the plebians find place in his society.

Man has been the perennial focus in any work of art. In the bourgeois novels, the primal feelings or views of the characters do not get the required attention. Lukacs says, "Man, for these writers, is by nature solitary, asocial, unable to enter into relationship with other human beings" ("The ideology of modernism" 476). Lukacs further establishes that any contact between individuals is either superficial or accidental. Basu's characters are not solitary beings as described by Lukacs; neither are they asocial. They bustle with activities and one can see love-hate relationship which results from human interaction, conflicts, and feuds in every novel. A scene in *Your Life to Live* is worth mentioning:

> Ladies woke up half an hour earlier than the men to get ready and look fresh. There was a queue for the use of bathrooms. "Hurry up", "Hurry up", were the words of the hour. Until the children went to school and the men went to work, every minute was important. There were eight or ten school-going children who were under orders to do their homework exactly between the hours of seven and nine. If they did their studying in silence there was danger of punishment. Rules were clearly laid down that voices must be heard. Pronunciation must be loud and clear. A chorus of children produced enough noise to drown the sound of the oil mill across the road. (126)

This passage proves the fact that Basu's people are full of human feelings. The characters wish to interact with the people young and old alike. This type of domesticity cannot be seen in Marxian writing. Basu's men and women do not fit into the Marxian frame of characters.

The requirements of a Marxist work are stated by Edmund Wilson in "Marxism and Literature":

(1) 'directly or indirectly show the effects of the
class struggle'; (2) 'the author must be able to make
the reader feel that he is participating in the lives
described'; and, finally, (3) the author's point of
view must 'be that of the vanguard of the proletariat; he should be, or should try to make himself,
a member of the proletariat'. (248)

When rules are laid and when an artist is expected to create works of art in accordance with the norms prescribed,
there can be no room for individuality. The subject of *Outcast* and *Blackstone* is, no doubt, class struggle, but Romen
Basu's treatment is different in the sense that he does not
approve of all the activities of the proletariat. In fact, he
presents the pros and cons of all the parties with an objectivity. There is an open comment on Congress men. Biresh
in *Outcast* says, "Congress has ruled our country for too
long without any opposition. We cannot tell the difference
between who is good and who is not, they all stink" (*Outcast* 51). In another instance Nelo passes belittling remarks
on the communist party: "They say the communists are
insincere, they promise a lot, but they do nothing. Congress atleast fulfils some of its promises" (*Outcast* 63). A
Marxist writer cannot allow this type of comment in his
work. In another situation, the Naxalites plan to blow up
the Shiva temple and Sambal joins that group in this ven-
ture. Putki is in doldrums: "She could live with him under
any conditions, if he cared to be reasonable and gentle
with her. He did not want her any more, she was convinced. If she meant anything to him, he could never go
ahead with his plans knowing they could never be together" (*Outcast* 244-245). Putki does not support terroristic activities which is clearly stated in the novel. A critical
study of *Outcast* underscores that Romen Basu shows no
allegiance to any party. In this context, what Lawrence
says of the genre of novel in general is quite significant: "If
you try to nail anything down, in the novel, either it kills
the novel, or the novel gets up and walks away with the

nail....When the novelist puts his thumb in the scale, to pull down the balance to his own predilection, that is immorality" ("Morality and the Novel" 128).

Henri Arvon discusses the role of the Marxist writer whom the capitalist society treats not as a creator but as a consumer and parasite on the one hand and producer on the other. The society permits him to make a living by the public scale of his work through sale of his time and labour. It also subjects him to alternating dependence and independence. By putting a creative writer on a par with a labourer, Henri Arvon states, "...the modern artist is deprived of any guarantee that the fruits of his own labour can satisfy a series of needs, if not urgent atleast extensive and regular enough in the market of supply and demand" (*Marxist Esthetics* 113). A Marxist writer is reduced to the state of a worker depending solely on the society. Basu belongs to a different class altogether: "I prefer to have one or two people understand and appreciate my message than masses of best seller, the reader who does not read or comprehend the meaning within the pages of a book" (lecture). His interest in the quality of the reader stands evidence to the fact that he is not a sheer propagandist.

George Orwell has objections against the language of a Marxist writer. He finds the political writing vague and incompetent. When discussing the language of the Marxist writing he feels:

> The jargon peculiar to Marxist writing (hyena, hangman, cannibal, petty bourgeois, these gentry, lackey, flunkey, mad dog, white guard etc.) consists largely of words and phrases translated from Russian, German or French; but the normal way of coining a new word is to use a Latin or Greek root with the appropriate affix and where necessary, the - ize for mation.

> ("Politics and the English Language" 363)

Basu's language is simple and clear, which does not exhibit any usage of Marxian language.

A great work of art is an orchestration where dialogue, characterization and narration combine to create a
parallel world with which one can compare his own world
and clearly learn if possible. The novel as a great work of
art has its own infrastructure. The plot of the novel is a
selection of events arranged in time, one event leading to
the other. For instance, Zarina, a Muslim, marries a Hindu
Arun, in *Your Life to Live*. Their religious differences added
with other misunderstandings end up in their separation.
Zarina believes that Arun is at fault and chooses to live
with her parents. She even wishes to resume her relationship with Professor Shukla, her idol and mentor during
her college days. There is a change in her thought-sequence
after hearing the miserable lives of her friends Mala and
Urmila Dutt. Comparing Arun with the husbands of her
friends she realises that after all he is not so bad. Her
realisation induces her to write to Arun: "I have seen prac-
tically all my friends gone over their lives. Truly I know
now that I do not deserve you....The separation has made
me wise" (176). On the other hand, Arun after meeting his
old friend Mrinal alters his opinion about Zarina. Mrinal
talks about misalliances: "One of the two wants to domi-
nate. Men are accused of being bullies or women are
frowned on for henpecking" (162). This conversation serves
as an eye opener and helps a reconciliation. The change of
their minds is well supported by convincing situations
which the plot warrants. As Marjorie Boulton says,
"...function of the plot is simply to provide pegs or shelv-
ing where the author can put things that he wishes to
display. His chief interest may be in characters and motive; but characters reveal themselves in action" (*The
Anatomy of the Novel* 48). Romen Basu formulates his plots
in such a way that the characters reveal themselves.

The plot decided, the novelist focuses his attention on
characters, major and minor. There are novelists who create plots for the sake of characters also. Basu's creativity
process seems different: "I begin with the title. The title

tells it all. I write basically for 'cause'. I don't write for amusement or to make the world wiser" (Interview). The novelist not only selects characters but gives varying degree of importance to his characters. He makes them types—spokesmen, symbols, and myths. Romen Basu's characters are basically Indian. They have a conversational Bengali tone. He sets forth a human story, warm and glowing through characterisation. There is a general opinion that his works appear to be translations of Bengali novels. But one must understand that the Indian characters with Indian flavour are more convincing. Meera Bose compliments on the realistic Indian atmosphere in *Outcast*:

> The boat ride of the two lovers brings a character-
> istic whiff of rural Bengal though Sambal's thoughts
> are elsewhere, Putki's brave venture into Calcutta
> and Writer's Building is credibly drawn, because
> her devotion to Sambal would give her the
> courage. The gatherings at Bhuban's tea shop are
> realistic and yet potent.

> (*The Literary Criterion* 78)

The characters can be 'flat' or 'round' as E.M. Forster defines. The test of a round character is that it must be capable of surprising in a convincing way. Mohamaya in *The Tamarind Tree* astonishes the readers convincingly. She accompanies Biren to the cremation ground at night to while away the time. She walks at ease because of the familiarity of the place and frequency of visits. Biren is jittery which he conceals lest he be called a coward:

> Suddenly he [Biren] had a feeling that Mohamaya
> was not beside him. The thought made him dizzy.
> When he turned around, Mohamaya was not there.
> He gave an agonized cry for her. Mohamaya came
> out from behind the lime tree and ran to him. Biren
> threw himself on her. She held him tight. His trem-
> bling quietened in her arms.

> (*The Tamarind Tree* 59)

What is more surprising about the character is that the

same Mohamaya feels dizzy in Biren's mansion in Calcutta. She sits in a corner confused by the strange surroundings:

> She worried how to find her way around in that sixty-room mansion. Suppose she got lost in one of the corridors, or got locked out on the roof?...That ferocious Alsatian dog chained near the gate—she shivered at the thought of being bitten at the wrist or neck. (124)

Mohamaya who roams fearlessly in cremation ground shivers in places where human beings inhabit. This sounds unnatural. Yet the character is a strange blend of individualism and ruralism, and so the reader is made to accept the peculiarity.

The character development is so handled by the novelist to suit his purposes. Some characters grow with the novel like Shakespeare's Hamlet, Flaubert's Madame Bovary and Hardy's Tess. The minor characters are either supporting characters or caricatures. In novels like *Outcast* and *A Gift of Love* the characters show steady growth and wholesomeness. Sambal in *Outcast* is a carefully moulded character who appears as a small boy witnessing the death of his father. That incident kindles the rebel in him. All the facets of his characters are displayed in the novel. He obeys the orders of mastermoshai: "We will give our lives for you, if you trust us, Mastermoshai" (*Outcast* 40). At the same time, he is not devoid of romance. To Putki, Sambal shows his undivided attention and love. He tells her, "I worry sometimes that you don't quite see how much I love you. If I am stubborn it does not mean that I love you less" (*Outcast* 231-232). The same Sambal, in the final scene, rejects Putki to fulfil his mission of life. When he rejects Putki the conversation between them explains the crucial condition:

> "...Is a woman's place in a man's life to be compared with his co-workers?"
>
> "These men are my two arms. They will give their

> lives for me without questioning. From you, all I
> get is resistance. You want me to be like the other
> rabbits in Basuli." (243)

In this process one finds that Sambal's character is ren-
dered true to life. Sambal grows in all dimensions throughout the novel. His interactions with people and society
reveal his character. Anand Raj Singh is all praise for Basu's
characterisation of Sambal:

> Most of the characters come alive in the book but
> that of Sambal has been well drawn out rounded
> and reasonably growing from small boy to young
> man full of idealism and raw vigour. He has never
> known fear and remains a living dynamite sparked
> into explosion several times causing blood to flow.

> (*The Pioneer* 15)

The credibility of a character is very important in
characterisation. It must be real, a blend of good and bad
characteristics. The problem of creating characters credibly
is a challenging task and a novelist encounters it when he
shapes the characters. No man in truth is good or bad in
entirety. Marjorie Boulton expresses this difficulty:

> A good character is more credible if he has some
> natural frailties as is a bad character if he has some
> glimmer of goodness, or wins some slight sympa-
> thy by a clue as to why he is bad. In the field of
> character, one of the hardest tasks is to create some-
> one good who is neither incredible nor insipid.

> (*The Anatomy of the Novel* 79)

The character which comes to one's mind in this context is
Parashar Ghose, the school teacher in *Outcast*. Parashar
risks his life in taking sides with Sambal. He tries his best
to unite Sambal and Putki in wedlock. He helps the untouchable school children. He not only imparts education
but buys books for poor children by collecting money from
others. His ambition proves to be his handicap. The villagers revere him: "He was neither dumb nor wicked, yet

why couldn't he see that boys and girls studying in the same school surely lead to immorality. In the end he got on everyone's nerves with his constant badgering for more money for this and that amenity for the school" (*Outcast* 209).

The school teacher reminds the village school master of "Deserted Village" in virtue and nobility:

> For e'en though vanquished, he could argue still,
> While words of learned length and thundering
>   sound;
> Amazed the gazing rustics ranged around;
> And still the gazed, and still the wonder grew,
> That one small head could carry all he knew.
>
> (*A Goldsmith Selection* 19-20)

The character of Parashar Ghose, the school teacher, is a realistic picture of the archetype of teachers.

The flat characters are constructed around a single idea or quality. The advantage of flat characters is that it is "easily recognised by the reader's emotional eye, not by the visual eye which merely notes the recurrence of a proper name" (*Aspects of the Novel* 74). Romen Basu uses the flat characters for his convenience. For instance, the zamindar Paramesh Ganguli in *Outcast* sets a panic-stricken atmosphere even before his appearance. Mahanta, an untouchable, enters the Kali temple and when he sees the zamindar with a group of men, he is horrorstruck. Even as the zamindar's voice is heard near the gate, fear grips him of the impending wrath. Mahanta feebly cries, "Zamindar babu coming to the temple at this hour of the night" (*Outcast* 5)? One can imagine how violently the zamindar will react to Mahanta's entry into the temple. The fear is felt even before the novelist begins to explain because the character speaks for itself. The zamindar is one of the tra-ditionally rich men—individually poor and yet posing to be rich. Such men are common sight in villages.

The consistency of the character is essential for its credibility. In the earlier novels of English literature the hero is consistent in his virtuosity. His modern counterpart is an admixture of heroic qualities and frailties. Marjorie Boulton confirms the modern view of consistency of character when she says:

> Consistency is a delicate matter, because none of us is fully consistent—We are creatures of moods, cycles, and competing priorities—but all of us are partly consistent. We can accept in a fictional character unusual behaviour due to shock; snapping of control under pressure; falling in love; unexpected riches or poverty; bodily or mental illness.
>
> (*The Anatomy of the Novel* 81-82)

Even when the consistency is broken, a convincing reason may save good characterisation. Romen Basu presents the modern hero as a blend of good and bad characteristics with convincing reasons.

Sukumal, the hero of *A Gift of Love*, has a heretic bent of mind. Ihab Hassan explains the essence of the anti-hero: "If the anti-hero seems now-a-days to hold us in his spell, it is because the deep and disquieting insights revealed to us by modern literature often require that we project ourselves into the predicament of victims" (*Radical Innocence* 21). The rubric of an anti-hero is stamped on Sukumal even as he is introduced in the police station when his father begs the police inspector to release him on bail. His overtures to Karuna, the neighbour girl and his gangster friends make him the black sheep of the family. Chhotopishima says: "He will influence the others, corrupt the better ones. He was possessed with evil power from the minute he was born. I know it from the Almanac that the day and hour he was born were most inauspicious" (*A Gift of Love* 15). Sukumal turns anew after he steps into the English soil. His search for love attracts him to Nell and then Shirley, a prostitute. Shirley's death brings him back to India, where he is endeared to Indu, a prostitute and then marries Kajali, the servant-maid's daughter. When one reads through the novel, Sukumal's problem with identity is obvious. Despite his aristocratic birth, he always associates himself with the lower classes. The author imputes this loss of identity to his motherlessness in a convincing way. The yearning for mother's love attracts him to the women who show genuine love and affection. His quest for love is explicit when he says: "I am attracted to women who can love unselfishly" (*A Gift of Love* 157). He sees a selfless mother in the prostitute whom the family and society condemn. The endeavours to fulfil his desires lead to estrangement. Ihab Hassan rightly refers to the alienation of the anti-hero:

> Society may modulate his awareness of his situation, but only existence determines his stand, the recoil of the modern self in its way of taking a stand. The retreat weakens its involvement in the living world. It leads it in the ways of violence and alienation, augments its sense of guilt and absurdity, and affords it no objective standard for evaluating the worth of human action.
>
> (*Radical Innocence* 31)

Viewed in this light Sukumal can be called an anti-hero. G.S. Balram Gupta writes in appreciation of Sukumal's characterisation:

> Although the novel is by no means lacking in variety of incidents (which keep the reader's eye constantly glued to the page before him) its real source of interest is the ceaseless flight of Sukumal (for that is the name of the narrator protagonist) to keep loneliness and frustrations at bay. Thrown on his own resources and emotionally cut off from everybody in the family from first to last he is passionately trying to reach out to others in his desperate longing for love and each time he feels let down.
>
> (*The Journal of Indian Writing in English* 68-69)

The courage and candour of a realist are seen in the

inhibitionless details in the process of Sukumal's upringing which speak for his anti-heroic bent of mind. Thus consistency turns a basic norm for Romen Basu's characters.

The backgound or the backdrop of the novel — what one calls the setting or the venue — can become a *sub-rosa* character as in Wordsworth and Waverley novels. The backdrop may reflect the mood of the scene as seen in Thagazhi's *Chemmeen*. Romen Basu's Calcutta is recurrent in almost all his novels. Except the last novel *My Own Witness* all his novels have Calcutta for their backdrop. Basu hailing from Bengal is able to provide convincing picture of Calcutta. Even the foreign countries which Basu pictures are presented very realistically and in a lively manner. Unless the author is thorough with the geography and the topography of the place, the details cannot be represented accurately. As Marjorie Boulton rightly says:

> The background of the novel does not consist just of scenery, which indeed is rarely of paramount interest, but of the whole environment: the country, district, urban or rural location, climate, data, customs, economic level, occupational groups, buildings, diet, family patterns, religion, politics, moral assumptions, intellectual and cultural life, education, amusements, standard of living and so on.
>
> (*The Anatomy of the Novel* 125-126)

The authenticity of the place described forms an important factor in the novel for which the first hand knowledge of the place is essential. The range of the artist determines the periphery of his expanse.

The range of the artist depends on the exposure which the artist is subjected to. Some artists widen their range by travelling and extensive reading. It is a known fact that Jane Austen's novels do not hint Napoleonic wars that were fought during her times. Her range is very limited within which she excelled. The Indian novelists such as

Mulk Raj Anand and Manohar Malgonkar do not extend their range. To a traveller like Romen Basu, sky is the limit. His characters include Italians, the French, Jews, Vietnamese and non-residential Indians as well as native Indians. A novelist cannot go beyond his range unless he is sure of his grounds. Romen Basu writes about all country men whom he is familiar with. His frequent world tours have exposed him to world cultures and so his characters are true to the country they belong. The Italian family with the native qualms of religious consciousness comes alive in *Portrait on the Roof*. Monsignor Contini represents the religious consciousness of the Italians when he says, "Science may take a long, long time to discover all the mysteries of the world. Until then, a little faith will go a long way" (129).

Candles and Roses has the backdrop of Parisian sensuousness with its gourmet restaurants and night clubs. The author seems to feel at home everywhere. He takes the readers around Paris by etching impressive vignettes that bear testimony to his minute observation. One such picture may be cited here:

> Usually Samir stopped in the Cafe de la Porte on Rue Balgere for coffee and *croissants*. Today, he decided he would go somewhere he could sit and enjoy the sun. He walked down Rue de Chateaubriand to the corner where the little grocery store displayed a tempting pyramid of huge, sweet Jaffa oranges. (1)

In addition to the accuracy of description of the place the author throws light on even the type of food available in the place he describes. Samir speaks of a type of wine called Hungarian Tokay: "A wine of romance and majesty. Voltaire praised it, Schubert sang of it, Louis XIV called it the wine of sovereigns and the sovereign of wines" (*Candles and Roses* 45). Even the description of the wine is poetic. A careful study of Basu's novels will reveal his knowledge about the country, its people, their way of life and their culture.

The events of the story *Hours Before Dawn* happen in three different continents — America, Asia and Europe. Mrinal and Kabita are world citizens. They always disagree about where they want to settle. Kabita says, "England is not my home, Daddy" (63). Mrinal has no intention of settling in India. He differs from her in his view on India: "After five years abroad he felt no real national spirit to draw him back to India. The country had so many opportunities to move rapidly but it was stifled by political disharmony, opportunism and each individual struggling for his own selfish ends" (*Hours Before Dawn* 68-69). The rootlessness that is typical of the non-residents is conspicuous in the speeches of Mrinal and Kabita. Romen Basu's range is not only wide but deep as well. The characters appear true to the soil, race and religion.

The Bengali household of Romen Basu gives ample scope for a galaxy of characters. In *A House Full of People* the author furnishes a family chart to avoid confusion in the relationship of characters. Every character is endowed with a unique characteristic to distinguish one from the other. Sudhin Roy is embodiment of nobility. Arun is the black sheep of the family. Chaya is the nagging wife of Karan. With this type of characterisation, the novelist manages a team of characters without difficulty.

Romen Basu's life has laid no limitations on travel and by ingenious choice, he extends his range to reach furthermore. His life abroad does not prevent him from presenting realistic pictures of India. The realistic pictures of Naxalite outbursts in his novels show his familiarity with the happenings in India. The demonstration of an outbreak in *Blackstone* is pictured with Indian touch and flavour:

> The brutal firing continued until everyone present
> prostrated themselves on the ground hiding their

faces: The sky looked black, the trees looked black, darkness had suddenly gripped the area. The police did not bother to count the victims, they are satisfied with the slaughter.

(*Blackstone* 72)

When asked about his portrayal of Indian scenes he replies with a ring of authenticity:

Siddharth Shanker Ray was the Chief Minister. I felt more saddened. He could not see beyond that this could lead to a revolution. My political views are very definitely in the side of the underprivileged. When my daughter was doing research, I stayed with her in a *dak* bungalow. I saw the conditions there. (Interview)

His frequent visits to India and the journals keep him informed of the happenings in India. Romen Basu takes utmost care to be informed of contemporary Indian political, social and economic scenes. In his latest novel, *My Own Witness*, Indian history during the times of Indira Gandhi forms the matrix of the novel. The story is in keeping with the historical events.

The time sequence in a novel is used as a technique for emphasizing a particular idea and also for effect. The dislocations, reversals and oscillations are used according to the discretion of the author to highlight or tone down a particular idea or event. What E.M. Forster says "...in the novel there is always a clock" (*Aspects of the Novel* 43), is true and the clock is set according to the whims and fancies of the novelist. Romen Basu uses a single forward movement in *A House Full of People*. In *Your Life to Live* the narration shows brief lapses of time here and there. In *Outcast* and *Blackstone* the author picks up events and arranges them to form a sequence. In *Hours Before Dawn* the clock is set twenty-five years back after the opening scene. Kabita and Mrinal celebrate their twenty-fifth wedding anniversary. The story reverses to their courting days from which it is a single onward movement covering twenty-five years of their matrimony. This makes the opening scene dramatic coupled with anticipation.

The dramatic opening of Shakespearean magnitude can also be seen in *Outcast*. The novel begins abruptly:

> Mahanta was bleeding from the nose and mouth. His eyes were so swollen, he could hardly open them while the sub-inspector interrogated him... Why had Mahanta entered the temple, knowing it was an unforgivable sin for an untouchable to go beyond the outside gate of the holy place? What had possessed him to throw a red hibiscus at the altar of Goddess Kali?   (*Outcast* 1)

The heartrending beginning hints at the theme of the novel. The questions that arise have to find answer in the novel.

Again in *Portrait on the Roof*, the novel begins with a happy family gathering and a celebration. They pose for a family photograph: "They were all there. One hundred and two of them. It was aunt Sabitri's idea that Mitra clan should get together atleast once before Grandmother bade them all farewell and joined Grandfather Dwarakanath in Kailash" (*Portrait on the Roof* 1). O.P. Sharma says in approbation: "The novel begins with an intimate and realistic description of a chaotic family gathering of about a hundred people to bid farewell to the grandmother, the family patriarch in the antique family mansion. It is reminiscent of Galsworthy's *Foresyte saga*" (*The Tribune* 7). There is a shift in the linear time. There are two forward and backward movements in this novel. S. Krishnan praises Basu's sense of time: "He captures effortlessly both the sense of time standing still and time passing by evocative descriptions of nature" (*The Hindu* 20). Romen Basu belongs to the clan of modern writers widening the perception of time like James Joyce and Virginia Woolf.

Except for the first person narrative in *A Gift of Love* all other novels follow the third person narrative where the author is omniscient. Regarding the first person narrative, the drawbacks and advantages are both equally balanced. Lubbock speaks about this type of narration:

> The characterized "I" is substituted for the loose and general "I" of the author: the loss of freedom is more than rapid by the more salient effect of the picture. Precision, individuality is given to it by this pair of eyes known and names through which the reader sees it; instead of drifting in space above the spectacle he keeps his allotted station and contemplates a delimited field of vision.
>
> (*The Craft of Fiction* 127-128)

Sukumal's narration of the story in the novel appears to be a device with the motive of the benefit in the sense that the picture has a definite edge. Its value is out to the best advantage. In addition to the field of vision, the quality of the tone is determined by the use of this type of narration. The hero or the narrator gives the story an indispensable unity by his narration. As the whole story belongs to one man, the ontological relationship is maintained.

Romen Basu's language is simple, crisp and direct. His language gives form to the content and perpetuates the theme. There are no long winding sentences, circumlocutions, which need intensive reading. Much of the story is conveyed through dialogue and the speech of the characters conveys the story.

Basu's language is often more business-like. Even the love-dialogue between Putki and Sambal is neither overlaid with emotions nor coquettish. Putki says to Sambal: "Do you know often I am called a whore because I am seen with you" (*Outcast* 27) to which Sambal plays cool: "Then you better stop seeing me, if you are afraid" (*Outcast* 27). Perhaps Basu deliberately uses an unromantic language for this ideology-obsessed couple.

In *Blackstone* Sombhu receives orders from the party to silence his father for expressing opposing views. When the readers anticipate a powerful language overlaid with emotions, the language tends to be unemotional:

> Sombhu walked up to him, knelt down and in the light of the streetlamp studied his shrunken face with its prominent cheekbones. His hand did not tremble, he did not shut his eyes. Raising his arm all the way back, he thrust the knife with full force into his father's chest, piercing his heart. Only a whimpering breath passed through the old man's nostrils. Sombhu wiped the blood stained knife on his father's shirt. (79)

The blood curdling action is expressed in simple language and style. The language is not emotion-packed probably because a Naxalite has to overcome emotions first. The language is suggestive of matter-of-fact like expression suitable to the character's ideals.

Romen Basu does not make much use of symbols except in two instances. In *A House Full of People*, the symbolic representation of the Roy family is done by the description of the old house with which the novel begins. The withering aristocracy of the house is indicated symbolically: "...the walls were full of cracks from which banyan trees sprouted. The house needed painting. It was a massive structure three storeys high" (*A House Full of People* 1). The symbolic depiction of the house conveys the real condition of the family including the remnants of the old pride.

In *The Tamarind Tree*, the tree strikes symbolic note when the novelist describes it:

> It was his [Anukul's] father who had planted that tamarind tree seventy years ago. That Tamarind tree was his favourite spot for rest or reading. Before he died he had asked Anukul to preserve the area and protect that tree. He had failed to honour his father's last wish. (18-19)

The place where the tree grows is the bone of contention between the two families. The feud ends with the marriage of Biren, Anukul's son, and Mohamaya. The village accepts the ownership of Anukul. While reading the novel one is reminded of the use of tree as a symbol by V.S. Naipaul in *Mr. Stone and the Knights Companion*. Mr. Stone looks at the tree in the school grounds at the back of his house:

> ...by which he noted the passing of time, the waxing and waning of the seasons, a tree which daily when shaving he studied, until he had known its every branch. The contemplation of this living object reassured him of the solidity of things....They were only a reminder of the even flowing of time, of his mountaining experience, his lengthening past. (16)

Arthur Miller, an American playwright, shows the physical presence of a tree on the stage which symbolises life, in "All My Sons". The characters mention the tree repeatedly and there is bitterness when Mother tells Georgie, "Did you see what happened to Larry's tree, Georgie" (Arthur Miller's *Collected Plays* 106)?

The technique of symbolising the tree by Romen Basu does not continue throughout the novel. As S. Krishnan states, "While the *Tamarind tree* makes a good title for his novel, its role as a symbol is not fully worked out" (*The Hindu* 21). Basu is not a symbolist though his formative influence includes American symbolists such as Faulkner, Saul Bellow and Hemingway.

The short stories of Romen Basu feature him as global writer. His merging of sensibilities, humour and compassion appear as basic virtues in the short stories. The wide canvas in the short story gives variety to his ideas. The anti-climax descends steeply and swiftly to make the narration interesting. The story of "A Professional Friend" ends with a sensuous and humorous denouement. Matoes picks up a friendship with Miranda and lures her to his desires. When he outsteps his limits she chokes him with a question: "I am a professional. You would't want a doctor friend of yours to treat you free, would you" (*Rustling of Many Winds* 143)? Dr. Ayyappa Panicker calls this anticlimax as 'O Henry Twist' in his review of Basu's short stories.

The concept of man as an individual is a topic of perennial interest and Romen Basu as an artist and individual shows the various influences of society on individual and individual on society. This concept becomes a technique in the hands of an artist and Romen Basu proves himself to be an artist. Lawrence explains the relationship between man and his environment:

> The business of art is to reveal the relation between man and his circumambient universe, at the living moment. As mankind is always struggling in the toils of old relationships, art is always ahead of the 'times', which themselves are always far in the rear of the living moment.
>
> (D.H. Lawrence "Morality and the Novel" 127)

An individual is a member of the society in isolation and his opposing self exists in the form of the society around him. As a result, the individual and the society vie with each other. In this eternal war the success of one side is not everlasting because the conditions do not remain the same. The society is powerful numerically and so the individual's victory is temporary or limited. The society also loses when a powerful individual arises as it happens infrequently. Romen Basu is aware of these interactions between the society and the individual and the interactions provide him with the themes.

The individual has a meek role to play in Indian society because the society is all powerful. With controlling factors like religion, caste, class and gender the individual is lost in the cross-currents of the omnipotent society. The Hindu society clings to religion with unquestioning faith and the religion controls their lives. The discriminations on the basis of the caste are practised with the specific or sometimes assumed sanction of religion.

According to the Act XXII of 1955, untouchability stands abolished giving a free access to the untouchables in places of worship, shops and restaurants. But the police inspector shouts at Mahanta: *"That's obvious, you son-of-a-pig. Had you no fear of punishment for walking up those holy steps, where you and your kind are debarred"* [Repeated for emphasis (*Outcast* 1)]? In a society which is caste-conscious, laws remain only within the pages of law books. Sambal who has been a witness and victim of all atrocities vouchsafes: "Seven years ago at the police station after seeing my father beaten, I took a vow that one day I would open the Kali temple door to everyone. No more would anyone fear a thrashing for being born untouchable" (*Outcast* 26). Sambal's words are not empty words because his later activities prove his war against the society.

The family, as a system, has its own regulations. The hierarchy and the rules and regulations within a family are more strict than the laws of the society. A joint living is made possible only at the expense of individual's choices and preferences. The elders lay down the rules and enforce them strictly. Any member who defies the rules in favour of his personal interests becomes a heretic in their eyes. There is no room for individual's likes and dislikes in the rigid households. It needs a lot of courage to establish the rights of an individual in matters of dress, food, way of life. Romen Basu with a deep attachment for the age-old joint family system is still aware of the individual's desires. He portrays heroes such as Arun and Ashoke who break open the shackles to prove themselves to be individuals. Arun in *A House Full of People* finds the western ways of life attractive. The freedom fascinates him and so he switches to western ways to the consternation of the family members. When he is questioned for coming home late he retorts: "I am over twenty-four years old and have a good job. I cannot be told when to come and when to go.

I know what I am doing" (21). The elders despise Arun's independent gestures but Arun shows his defiance by violating the authority of the elders.

Ashoke in *Your Life to Live* is an improvement on Arun who shows a love of adventure. He loves freedom of all sorts. Having been born in a joint family he observes the difference between western and eastern ways of life. His preference tilts in favour of western life because of the unlimited freedom enjoyed by the people. His love of freedom is obvious when he says:

> I believe in free enterprise. I believe that man's ambition should not have any limits. He can achieve anything he wishes if he tries hard at it. Under the American system everybody has an equal chance. Because of their democratic ways, because of their value for merit, I as an Indian am unable to work here. (74)

Ashoke's protests are shown in the form of hard work even during his education in order to earn, save money and to leave India, in search of his freedom and independence. Ashoke leads a totally independent life in America where society does not impose strictures on him.

Sukumal's boyhood days are painful because he does not adhere to the rules of the house. All his activities are against the rules of the family and society. The result is severe punishments from family members: "If I fall in the hands of one of my uncles, I got hit on the head, caned on the palm of my hand or had my ears twisted. *Boropishima* did not wish to get involved in anything, least of all with me, but *Chhotopishima* was exactly the opposite. She hounded me whenever there was a chance" (*A Gift of Love* 18). Punishments do not alter his independent spirit and he feels that people who are obedient are lifeless: "The other cousins were like vegetables — they just obeyed their parents and were good; always afraid of punishment" (18). Sukumal's adventurous boyhood spirit continues. He loves prostitutes and marries the daughter of a servant-maid

amidst protests. Basu's heroes in general are out of ordinary and freedom lovers. They break the social order by
their speech and action.

Basu's heroines and women characters are also more
individualistic than his male characters. The family expects
implicit obedience and discipline from women. The woman
is expected to perform her duties. She has to attend to the
husband, children and other family members without expecting anything in return. They must be well versed in
household arts such as cooking, sewing and embroidery.
Mohamaya, the heroine of *The Tamarind Tree*, is not 'feminine' or 'womanly'. She goes about singing devotional
songs. No one can exhort her to go against her instincts.
When she is married, the ladies try to bring her under
their control. The lady by making enquiries comes to know
of the boisterous nature of Mohamaya. She only accuses,
"You expected to get married into a rich home, so there
was no need for you to enter the kitchen" (122)?
Mohamaya's behaviour surprises the ladies but she does
not alter her ways. She is unable to fit into the family and
so returns to her parents. Instead of changing her ways
she comes to the place where she can continue to live her
own way.

Putki in *Outcast* shares the qualities of Mohamaya.
She is beyond correction. Her love for Sambal is not encouraged because he belongs to the lowest class of untouchables: "She had defied her father to continue seeing
her childhood friend. He (Her father) had confined her
without food or water for three or four days at a time. She
had been whipped until permanently scarred when she
had disobeyed and been found speaking to Sambal" (*Outcast* 27). This proves her mettle and stubborn nature. She
shows the same courage when Sambal is in prison. With
the help of Parashar Ghose she bails him out. Putki's individuality is in action whenever the society is against her.

In *Blackstone* Kalapathor's anger turns into rage when
his only sister Futu is raped by two policemen. Two po-

licemen come to the home of Kalapathor's disguised as women. They blindfold Futu and take her to an abandoned house. They rape her and cut her body to slices. Her mutilated body is found feeding the vultures the next day. Kalapathor conveys this horrifying experience to Mukul with a sympathetic note: "Perhaps you can understand now why I want death for those policemen" (*Blackstone* 54). Kalapathor becomes a revolutionary after seeing his father murdered and sister raped and dismembered. In Mulk Raj Anand's *Untouchable* there is a similar occurrence but the reaction of the individual is passive. Sohini, Bakha's sister, is given water by the temple priest only to lure her to feed his sensual desires. When Bakha raises his voice for justice, the whole village turns against Bakha's sister for polluting the temple while the priest's act goes unquestioned. Bakha could only cry, "Why was she born so beautiful in a low caste family" (*Untouchable* 54)? Mulk Raj Anand's hero resigns to his lot meekly while Basu's hero takes cudgels against the adversary. Kalapathor's revenge against the upper class society results from the injustice meted out to him. Romen Basu shows that an individual force can also act powerfully against the society.

Even Basu's minor characters show individualistic trend. They contribute to the cause and resist the society if necessary. The characters work for harmony in family and society. Saraju, a widow in *Outcast*, is placed before the Gram Panchayat with the charge of adultery. She expresses her defiance by refusing to cover her head. Even when she is questioned unjustly she faces the interrogation calmly which is unlikely in the case of a woman of lower class. She admits eating meat with men but when her morals are questioned she bluntly repudiates the accusation. Saraju stands out from other characters by her individualistic traits. She is, perhaps, the new woman in the offing.

Alpana in *The Street Corner Boys* is a unique personality who does not conform to the rules of the family and society. She is a member of the royal family by birth and

marriage. Her marital life is no impediment to her political
career. Ghonu appreciates her levelheadedness:

> She married Pradita [sic] out of concern for him,
> but never tried to swallow him in her political life.
> You should see how they live. A devoted mother,
> modest wife, dutiful daughter-in-law, all that when
> she is at home. But not a shred of compromise
> with her movement and she does not bring her
> politics home. (151)

When compliments of such kind issue forth from one character about the other, Basu's unconscious support is
directed towards those characters and their character traits.

An individual, who flouts the tradition, be it man or a
woman, anticipates excommunication from the family.
Romen Basu's heroes and heroines are stubborn and resist
the family and society. Zarina a Muslim loves Ashoke a
Hindu in *Your Life to Live*. Her doting mother cannot approve of this marriage. She disowns Zarina: "Since you
have decided to marry him, you have taken the future in
your hands. I want you to know that from here on you
had better not try to keep any contact with us" (*Your Life to
Live* 51). This threat does not prevent her marriage with
Ashoke. She is prepared for ostracism from both family
and society.

Sukumal opens the topic of marriage to his father and
he is aware of what is in store for him. When his father
learns that his son's preference rests with the servant-maid's
daughter, he is worried about the response of the society.
Knowing the obstinacy of his son he says helplessly, "You
are very strong-headed. Once you decide to do something,
nothing can stop you. I beg you to give up this madness. I
have no objection to your choosing your own wife, but for
God's sake, do not disgrace us this way" (*A Gift of Love*
174). Sukumal's brother reproaches him. Even the servants
do not approve of this marriage though a person from
their class is lifted up in status. Amidst all protests
Sukumal's tenacity succeeds.

Basu's heroes and heroines prove themselves to be radicals who cannot be chained by religion, caste and tradition. By placing the individuals against the society he depicts their struggles to move against the current of the society. The characterisation has produced such an effect that the cause remains implicit and the harmony explicit.

Chapter 5

Summation

> *And here lies the vast importance of the novel, properly handled. It can inform and lead into new places the flow of our sympathetic consciousness, and can lead our sympathy away in recoil from things gone dead. Therefore, the novel properly handled can reveal the most secret places of life; for it is in the* passional *secret places of life, above all, that the tide of sensitive awareness needs to ebb and flow, cleansing and refreshing.*
>
> (D.H. Lawrence *Lady Chatterley's Lover* 92)

Human relationship as a psychological study forms the basis of a novel. The novelist is interested in human relationship because novel is a book of life. The novelist creates characters that are true to life and the interaction between characters is based on a thorough knowledge of human relationship as determined by many factors — culture, race, sex, economy, power, status etc. The study of man and the complexities of human mind opens new vistas in the field of novel. The author's minute observation of life helps him in moulding the characters. Romen Basu, a traveller and an internationalist, with a better exposure to the behavioural patterns constructs plots constituting suitable themes and characters.

A House Full of People is a microcosm of a family where criss-cross relationships are maintained. Sudhin Roy, the eldest of the family, preserves the family honour by his kindness, sacrifice, tolerance and understanding. His inter-action with the members of the family is based on the knowledge of human understanding and relationship. He sacrifices his money, energy and time for the upkeep of the family. He chides the children when they go wrong or commit mistakes. The brothers differ in temperaments and his relationship with them varies accordingly. In his death-bed he compliments his wife on her adjustability: "You are the best thing that has happened to me. Without you, I could not have done any of the things that you say I have done. It is your understanding that has helped to keep the family together" (*A House Full of People*). The microscopic canvas can contain only miniature picture, but they have life in their own way. The mutual appreciation of wife by the husband explains how the old couple have served as the backbone of the family.

The love-hate relationship expounded by D.H. Lawrence is true to life. Romen Basu shows a mother and daughter in *Your Life to Live* whose feelings can be under-stood by every reader. Zarina in *Your Life to Live* chooses to marry a Hindu boy against her mother's wishes. The extreme love of the mother turns to bitter hatred. The mother stops all social interactions and indulges in self-denial. She who cherishes dreams about her daughter is unable to approve of her marriage with a Hindu. Zarina's father accounts for the reason: "It was extreme love for you that had turned into hatred" (*Your Life to Live* 103). He continues:

> In one corner of the boundary wall there was a pomegranate tree. She made a fenced wall with straw mats around the tree to hide herself from outside viewers. There she stayed most of the day. Lack of nourishment and loss of sleep have taken its toll. She looks like a bag of bones. (104)

The mother whose wishes have been turned down by the

daughter is bound to experience this animosity and Basu presents the situation realistically.

The jealousy between brothers for ownership of property is common in families. When no party is prepared to give in, discontentment results in the family. They harp on their prestige and end up in court. Gobindo a character in *The Tamarind Tree* sums up the cause of family feuds:

> My dear boy, in our society, honour is everything. The richer the man, the bigger is his ego. How do you suppose so many zamindars were wiped out? By fattening the lawyers. Brothers would rather watch their estates dwindle to zero than settle out of Court their quarrels over two mango trees or a sliver of a paddy field. (38-39)

The common sights and experiences related with exactitude bear evidence to the author's observation and understanding.

Basu's acquaintance with world cultures manifests in the form of pen pictures when it comes to the matter of man-woman relationship. Having come across men and women of several countries his dealings with their problems show universality. Ashoke and Zarina are Indians settled in the United States of America. They blend in themselves cultures of east and west. They are unable to resolve the clash of cultures and when their marriage reaches the breaking point Ashoke's friend Mrinal is analytical:

> No matter what the race, religion, caste, creed, wealth or education, there is one thing common to every man-woman relationship....If people are not able to see beyond their own need, no amount of passion could hold them together.
>
> (*Your Life to Live* 162)

The problem of human relationship is complex and Basu's approach conveys the complexities of the human mind as found in human beings. Kabita and Mrinal represent 'Man' and 'Woman' of the species when love becomes jealousy.

Love-hate relationship intrudes in Man-Woman relationship and Basu's characters enact it.

Male-chauvinism is one of the factors that affects man-
woman relationship. Man is unyielding and he expects the
woman to compromise. When woman is enterprising, jealous feelings draw them apart. Ashoke accepts his jealousy
in a proud manner: "Yes, I am a jealous man. I want the
whole world to know it. What man is worthy of woman's
love if he is not jealous of her" (*Your Life to Live* 175). The
Indian man demands the undivided, undiluted love and
attention from the woman. Zarina comments on his jealousy: "You want to put me in a cage as your favourite
'myna'. Feed me and talk to me when you come home and
when you ask me to whistle I must whistle" (60). A thin
line divides jealousy from love and love from hate and
Basu draws it accurately for the portrayal of his characters.

Psychological studies convey that incompatibility is a
cause for jealousy which breaks families. Even a mild sus-
picion is sufficient to kindle the embers of jealousy. Mrinal
misunderstands the friendship between his wife Kabita and
a young man Bose. Jealousy is born out of extreme love
and male-chauvinism acknowledges it with pride. Mrinal
universalises the jealousy of man when he says, "All men
are jealous, some admit it and the others lie about it"
(*Hours Before Dawn* 194). They do not come to terms with
life throughout the novel although one loves the other.
Mrinal's jealousy stems from his love and the Indian in
him accentuates the jealousy. The nuances of human relationship are well brought out in Basu's novels.

Misunderstanding among acquaintances is a common
phenomenon, as a part of human relationship. Any change
in the attitude of the characters is supported by a valid
reason to convince the readers. Based on this truth, the
novelist bases his characters and draws his themes. Kesab
who considers Kalapathor to be "... the most courageous,
loyal and trustworthy follower" (*Blackstone* 10), changes

opinion in due course. His revised opinion gets revealed
when Kesab says, "But I am forced to conclude that our
differences come from age and experience" (*Blackstone* 119).
The political allegiance also can serve as the cause for
revising opinion. When Kalapathor shifts his loyalty, Kesab
is forced to react differently because the party expects it.
Kesab's personal preference for Kalapathor does not interfere with his political activities. Pramila Lewis writes in
appreciation of their loyalties:

> The response of each of these men to the crisis is
> finely worked out in the context of the different
> temperaments, compulsions and cultural back-
> ground of each. The tension between loyalty to the
> party, the blind discipline demanded by it and the
> more down to earth instincts of the peasants and
> tribals who realise from their own experience that
> "loyalty" and "discipline" cannot be blind, is nicely
> drawn.
>
> (*Patriot* 10)

Romen Basu looks at the society with the objectivity of an
internationalist. He does not look at the world through
the eyes of a communist or a traditionalist. In *The Street
Corner Boys* the novelist seems to feel sorry for the crumbling tradition and traditional values under the influence
of modernity. The author's vision for a harmonious existence is revealed in the novel:

> Tarun was convinced that modernity does not have
> to destroy traditional values. Why could they not
> co-exist? Why couldn't the people have choice? The
> capitalist will invent new things for new markets.
> The communist will struggle for new recruits and
> new economic order.
>
> (*The Street Corner Boys* 141)

Tarun's view of life is modern and traditional simultaneously. Basu like Tarun aims at a life that is beyond political parties. Rather he wishes all the political parties to
unite together for the welfare of the society. The author

does not wipe out the possibilities of different parties but complementary working of different parties appears to be his ideology as it works out in the joint family system.

The trans-cultural panorama is possible only when there is a blending of cultures. In at least three of his novels, juxtaposition and contraposition can be seen. Unlike other novelists who differentiate between the occident and the orient, Romen Basu is able to see similarities between the west and the east. In *Candles and Roses* a French family is juxtaposed to an Indian family. Francis, a Frenchman, remarks in defence of the morale of the French girls:

> It's not 'free love', for all the talk there is about it. French girls don't go to bed with a man the first time they meet him or the second. They are conscious of their reputations and their family name. In France, the family is everything, as in India. (85)

When the general trend is either aping the west or condemning the western culture, Romen Basu with a ring of authenticity writes about cultural unity.

In *Portrait on the Roof* the story traverses the densely populated joint family of the Mitra clan in Calcutta and the distant ethos of Signor Lucian's family in Italy. The omniscient writer's words appear to be the authorial point of view:

> He had found that other Indians who went overseas either changed identity or condemned every thing they found different. For him, the differences were so few and the similarities so many that he could not accept that understanding could not be reached. (52)

Basu ignores the barriers of religion, language and race. He is an Indian and an internationalist simultaneously. His attitude towards sex and marriage and man-woman relationship does not lie within the narrow confines of tradition and orthodoxy.

Regarding marriage, Basu's idea seems to differ from the traditional marriages. In *A House Full of People* Reba's marriage is extravagantly planned despite the shrinking resources. The marriage is celebrated with such a pomp but the narration is infused with sarcasm when the financial problem of the Roy family is mentioned:

> What a fabulous wedding! It was true to the reputation of the Roy family. The dinner was lavish, the decorations exquisite and the dowry! No one knew how anyone could afford such luxury these days, especially the Roy family who were supposed to be having financial difficulties. (94)

These lines show that what is involved in the marriage is the prestige of the family and money is wasted in conducting the marriage in a grand way. Traditional marriage is praised in a mocking tone. This traditional marriage serves as a foil to the love marriage of Ranjith and Chithra in which Ranjith swears, "When I married you, I made it my life's desire to make you happy and find my happiness in whatever you chose to do" (*A House Full of People* 148). The lovers have personal commitment to marriage which is missing in the traditional marriage. A careful reader can realize that the novelist is sympathetic towards love marriage. Romen Basu is aware of the difficulties encountered by lovers in the Indian society, yet he seems to welcome marriage for love. Basu's heroes and heroines are united by love. They fight their way to marriage because society's impediments are hard. The harmony in the marital life is another aspect of life which should be considered important. Hence, his staunch support.

There is no inhibition on the part of the writer when he speaks about sex. His interview assures this idea: "I do believe that sex is the most beautiful thing in life as D.H. Lawrence has compared sex with religion. I am not a religious person to see how it has been a religious deliverance....Sex is very important element in the personal fulfilment of a person's life. I am not going to Freud or Jung. It is truth. For various reasons we inhibit it and keep our contentment elsewhere in the temples, churches and mosques" (Interview).

Sukumal in *A Gift of Love* not only indulges in masturbation but teaches the same to his cousin Babon. They are caught during this act and suffer punishment in the hands of *Chhotopishima*. She complains about Sukumal corrupting Babon's mind. Sukumal's father, after hearing her complaints, replies unperturbed: "Don't be so naive. Children learn these things at a certain age. If it was not Sukumal, it would have been someone else. Besides, it is not such a terrible thing" (*A Gift of Love* 21). The instincts which are generally prohibited from writing, especially by the Indian writers are dealt with casually. The author's wide travel and scientific knowledge might have contributed to this attitude of life.

Samir in *Candles and Roses* possesses independent ideas free from convention, tradition and orthodoxy. He marries Pramila and even when he finds that she is not willing to comply with his sexual desires, he does not regret the marriage. All the same, he does not feel guilty about living with Monique, a French woman who adores him. Extramarital sex is a sin and a taboo in India. But Samir is not guilty-conscious. His speech with Monique confirms his attitude:

> All I understand is that you spoil the true enjoyment of sex with all your inhibitions. No to this. No to that. Unless you can free yourself from any sense of shame, you will not be liberated. (79)

Prema Pandurangan is hostile about the characterisation of Samir:

> In some places, discussions both on art and religion remain a patchwork rather than an integral part of the plot. To an unsympathetic critic they even appear pedantic. Hinduism is more a matter of experience than exposition. The hero talks more

than what he practises. The roses are beautifully
red. Wish the candles burned bright.

(The Hindu Madras 15)

However, the researcher feels that the polarities in the character are treated convincingly. Samir's independent thinking and inhibitionless attitude to sex, religion and life gives him the liberation. The liberated mind is the uniqueness in his character.

Romen Basu's men and women are inhabitants of the modern world, hence they share the complexities of the age. The theme of man-woman relationship as sexual perversion and sadism is seen in *A Gift of Love*. Shirley's experience as a prostitute is horrifying:

> It took several visits before I could be naked in his presence. I wanted to switch off the light; he put an extra fiver on the bed to keep the light on. He then took out a whip, thin as a rope, from his topcoat pocket and said not to worry. He would whip me only as much as I could take in the beginning, then increase it each week....Each night's experience was unique. I began to wonder whether there were any normal, healthy men left in Britain who wanted normal, healthy sex. Was it the war that had deranged people mentally and physically? (115)

Shirley's experiences, bitter and horrid, reflect the intricacies of the human relationship in general and man-woman relationship in particular.

The author has a thorough knowledge of Hindu scriptures on which Hindu culture is founded. He ignores superstition and orthodoxy in the religion and recommends the good practices of Hindu philosophy. Samir tries to explain the complex Hindu philosophy in simple parlance:

> Anything that is real never changes. Alliance of the
> self with the universe comes when the mind does
> not desire or grieve or reject....But once one has
> attained true liberation, has become one with the

> universe, we believe that person will never be re-
> born, that his search is over.
>
> (*Candles and Roses* 55)

Samir's discourse on religion reflects on the author's religious accomplishments. O.P. Sharma compliments the
author's efforts: "The dramatic tension between the two
conflicting traditions, families, religions and ethnic back-
grounds is sharply drawn with meaningful dialogue
centring on family and religion" (*The Tribune* 7). Romen
Basu's novels endorse the notion that his interest is directed towards peaceful, harmonious existence in religion,
sex, marriage, family and society.

The nomenclature of *Outcast* denotes a larger perspective of the author against the smaller periphery of outcaste.
The deletion of the alphabet 'e' may be interpreted as the
author's concern in dealing with the outcast which means
'One who is cast out of society or home; anything rejected,
eliminated or cast out' (Chambers' Twentieth Century Dictionary). The term 'Outcaste' simply means 'one who is of
no caste or has lost caste' (Chambers' Twentieth Century
Dictionary). The complexity involved in the word 'Outcast' adds several layers of meaning to the novel. Sambal
in addition to being an outcaste is a social reject since he is
unable to come to terms with the society. He ends up as an
outcast because of his failure in fulfilling his life's mission.
One may assert that Basu in his quest for harmony lays
stress on his ideal of harmony by highlighting the negative
consequences of the same ideal. That is to say, Sambal
owing to his inability to act in harmony with the society is
more an 'Outcast' than 'Outcaste'. The title in its meaning
and logic is aptly chosen to fit the purpose of the novelist.

In addition to working for world peace and harmony
by lending his services to the United Nations Organisation,
Romen Basu has written novels for the same cause. *Sands
of Time* is a documentary novel in which the United Nations Organisation is the protagonist. His experiences with

the Organisation culminate in the form of a novel. Jacques says, "Heaven only knows when all the fires in the world will be put out, or if they ever will. But my generation will have to work relentlessly for the values we cherish from within this Organisation" (*Sands of Time* 15). In this novel the cause of the Jews is taken up as a major theme. Romen Basu's interest in the cause of the minority on the universal level is obvious. Tamara, a Jew, loses all her family members in Hitler's massacre of the Jews. She joins the United Nations hoping to get solace and consolation. She meets Ustum, a Muslim, falls in love with him that ends in marriage. After marriage she realises that she has made a wrong choice because he does not share her feelings for the Jews. Ustum accuses her of her Jewish sensitivity:

> Since our marriage, I have been sick to death hearing of what Hitler did to you and your lot. You have nothing to talk about except how badly you are treated because you are a Jew. Do the rest of the underprivileged go around moping all the time about how others hate them? Everytime we disagree, your problem as a Jew is behind it.

(Sands of Time 35)

The characters make all efforts to be above the national prejudices and cultivate a world-view, liberal enough to embrace the entire mankind. But when they are faced with doubts and uncertainties they do not know how to resolve them. Tamara is caught in the web of her racial encumbrances. She dissolves the marriage and when Bill proposes to her, she is apprehensive about making a second trial. She tells pathetically: "I was married once, my heart is deeply bruised, my childhood reminiscences give me pain most of the time, war has left its legacy of nightmares, and now I find Jews are outcasts, even in America. I have thought it over very seriously" (*Sands of Time* 144). Tamara's problem is perennial because human beings refuse to forget the differences. The author symbolises the racial

atrocities and its ill effects through the character of Tamara.
V.K. Joshi eulogises his efforts: "...he has been singularly
successful in focussing our attention on issues that are important for the survival of mankind and should not be
overlooked" (*Patriot* 15).

This novel shows how the people struggle to fit into a
system and the way they wish to effect a change. In this
process they experience a conflict between the individualistic policy and the institutional morals. The idealistic
motivation of men and women is frustrated; however, they
are convinced that they have carried out some mission.
The author's mission appears to be the mission of the in-
terns of the novel as well. As a visionary Romen Basu
dreams of an Utopia when people will unite together ig-
noring all their differences. Bill answers Tamara: "When
mankind realizes that human resources will outrun nature's
gifts and technology will ultimately threaten humans,
people will come to terms with one another" (*Sands of Time*
114). Basu's ultimate aim appears to bring the whole hu-
manity together. His characters voice his opinion. There
are suggestions in the novel as to how to bring about global peace. The character of Bill suggests a solution: "The
next Secretary-General should be a futurist, someone who
has a global view of human problems like the use of outer
space, sharing the wealth of the oceans, protecting the
world's environment, cross-cultural relations, religious
movements" (121).

These arguments speak for the universalism of Basu.
His concern extends beyond the family, the society to the
universe. He foresees the endangering power and order.
These are matters for universal consideration where and
when world nations ought to put their heads together to
come to universal consensus. The quest for harmony that
begins with the family extends to the universe.

Romen Basu as a living writer and promising author
with progressive ideas shows wide scope for further

research. The critics have not worked on him and any researcher can see a fund of themes worth research in his novels. Basu is a poet as well as a short story writer in addition to being a novelist. His short story collections reveal a sense of humour which may not be predominantly found in his novels. The variety of themes, multiple locale bestow on him the credit of being a good short story writer.

Basu's themes are Indian even if the setting is abroad. His deft fingers bring out the hues and smells of a foreign land while his themes and subject reflect Indianness. He says that all his books are published in India though his readers are mostly Americans.

Basu's earlier novels explore the familial relationship. Later novels establish him as a sociological writer. The east-west encounter is a topic constituting diverse elements. With increasing immigration and emigration, the relevance of cultural conflicts, and a need for cultural harmony is evident. One can analyse Basu's novels in these perspectives. With basic search for harmony at all levels, the author pursues on all directions. Regarding the future publications Basu says that a book on feminism is in progress. His 'Memoirs', a collection of poems, is yet to be published. The forthcoming publications may throw new light on the author.

There is art in Basu's writings. There is variety in his fiction. It is strange that not much critical material has gone into Basu's writings. What impresses one in Romen Basu is his fine blending of tradition and individuality. Essentially, he is a story teller though the 'cause' is equally important for him. There is no basic contradiction because the story and the cause merge resulting in a sociological novel. For instance both in *Outcast* and *Blackstone*, if Basu had not highlighted the personal agony of either Sambal or Kalapathor both the novels would have been mere documentary novels propagating rebellion and bloodshed. Now they become 'slices of life' — the injustice meted out to Sambal or Kalapathor could happen to any untouchable. This makes the novels at once personal and universal.

With all claim for objectivity in fiction one cannot deny the fact that some autobiographical elements can be gleaned. A study of Romen Basu's fiction chronologically reveals the fact — at least in a broader sense — he begins with the family — microlevel universe — and ends up with the society which is the macrocosm of the universe. As a committed and sensitive writer he is impatient with the atrocities inflicted upon the lower classes. A sarcastic remark about the Goddess makes the readers feel that there is no wonder that the people fight among themselves. The Morol tells the Zamindar: "...when Kali wanted to destroy the earth, because her father had spoken poorly of her husband, our Lord (Shiva)" (*Outcast* 185). One has to compare this scene with the stoic endurance practised by Onkar Singh which suggests that Basu has come to accept the reality with the sense of resignation if not serenity.

Because of his international experience, he has acquired a sense of understanding which helps him to present the superstitious Indian *milieu* and the mechanised materialistic atmosphere as well. Tennyson's Ulysses makes a pertinent claim:

> I am part of all that I have met;
> Yet all experience is an arch where thro'
> Gleans that untravelled world whose margin fades
> For ever for ever I move.

(*English Verse* 94)

Unlike Ulysses, Basu has not shed his Indianness. In a short story "A Glass of Water" the conversation between two old ladies is pathetic:

"Why do our children feel we are their liability? We cannot change their lives anymore."

"Old people are too old-fashioned for them."

"We cannot stop loving our families because we are old."

"They cannot understand that because they are young."

(*Rustling of Many Winds* 64)

When he presents the old women, he writes it without comments. One cannot miss the sub-text which is his spontaneous sympathy for old people. That is why, probably, he goes all out to defend the joint family system which is gradually dying out in India. It is this sympathy that leads to the tolerance of exploitation of elder brother and eldest son. The merits of the joint family-familial harmony with the sentimental attachment as the backdrop are worth any sacrifice according to him.

Basu differs in his treatment of society in an objective manner. On the societal level, the social injustice according to Basu is both predetermined and inhuman. Hence, the ruthless and bloody crusade against the social inequalities in the sociological novels. The man and the artist in Basu have attained maturity in the form of Onkar Singh who recommends religious tolerance which is the only solution in the context of Ayodhyas and Babri Masjids.

Works Cited

Primary Sources

Basu, Romen. *A House Full of People*. Calcutta: Navana, 1968.

—————. *Canvas and the Brush*. Calcutta: Firma K.L. Mukhopadhyay, 1971.

—————. *Your Life to Live*. Calcutta: Firma K.L. Mukhopadhyay, 1972.

—————. *A Gift of Love*. Calcutta: Lake Gardens, 1974.

—————. *The Tamarind Tree*. Calcutta: Lake Gardens, 1975.

—————. *Candles and Roses*. New Delhi: Sterling Publishers, 1980.

—————. *Portrait on the Roof*. New Delhi: Sterling Publishers, 1980.

—————. *Rustling of Many Winds*. New Delhi: Sterling Publishers, 1982.

—————. *Sands of Time*. New Delhi: Sterling Publishers, 1985.

—————. *Outcast*. New Delhi: Sterling Publishers, 1986.

—————. ed. *Reflections: Twenty One Indian Short Stories*. New Delhi: Facet Books International, 1989.

—————. *Hours Before Dawn*. New Delhi: Sterling Publishers, 1988.

—————. *Blackstone*. New Delhi: Sterling Publishers, 1989.

——————. *The Street Corner Boys*. New Delhi: Sterling Publishers, 1992.

——————. *My Own Witness*. New Delhi: Facet Books International, 1993.

Secondary Sources

Anand, Mulk Raj. *Coolie*. New Delhi: Mayfair Paperbacks, 1985.

——————. *Untouchable*. London: Hutchinson International Authors Limited, 1947.

Arvon, Henri. *Marxist Esthetics*. trans. from French by Helen R. Lane. Ithaka and London: Cornell University Press, 1973, 84-92.

Berreman, Gerald D. "The Brahminical View of Caste." *Social Stratification*. Ed. Dipankar Gupta. Delhi: Oxford University Press, 1991.

Bose, Meera. "*Outcast* — A Review." *The Literary Criterion*. 22.1 (1987): 71-79.

Boulton, Marjorie. *The Anatomy of the Novel*. London: Routledge & Kegan Paul, 1975.

Chellappan, K. "Voice in Exile: 'Journey' in Raja Rao and V.S. Naipaul." *Reworldling: The Literature of the Indian Diaspora*. Ed. Emmanuel S. Nelson. New York: Green Wood Press, 1992. 25-33.

Chinmayananda Swami. *The Bhagavad Geetha*. New Delhi: Mrs Sheila Puri, n.d.

Deshpande, Shashi. *Roots and Shadows*. Madras: Sangam Books, 1992.

Forster, E.M. *Aspects of the Novel*. Middlesex England: Penguin Books, 1927.

Frost, Robert. "Death of the Hired Man." *American Literature 1890-1965: An anthology*. New Delhi: Eurasia Publishing Pvt. Ltd., 1965.

Ghurye, G.S. *Caste and Race in India.* Bombay Popular Prakashan, 1979.

Gupta, G.S. Balram. "A Gift of Love." *The Journal of Indian Writing in English.* 5.2 (July 1977): 68-69.

Gupta, Dipankar. "Hierarchy and Difference: An Introduction." *Social Stratification.* Ed. Dipankar Gupta. Delhi: Oxford University Press, 1991. 1-21.

Hassan, Ihab. *Radical Innocence: Studies in the Contemporary American Novel.* New York: Prentice-Hall, Inc., 1968.

Iyengar, K.R. Srinivasa. *Indian Writing in English.* Bombay: Asia Publishing House, 1962.

Isaacs, Harold R. *India's Ex-Untouchables.* New York: Harper Torch Books, 1964.

Jeffares, Norman A. ed. *A Goldsmith Selection.* London: Macmillan & Co. Ltd., 1963.

Jhabvala, Ruth Prawar. *The Nature of Passion.* London: Penguin Books, 1986.

Joshi, V.K. "Enduring Moments of Life." *Patriot.* 15 December 1985.

Karve, Irawathi. *Kinship Organisation in India.* Deccan College Monograph Series No. 11. Poona: Deccan College, 1953.

Krishnan, S. "*The Tamarind Tree*: A Review." *The Hindu.* 27 April 1976. 21.

Lawrence, D.H. *Lady Chatterley's Lover.* London: The New English Library Ltd., 1932.

—————. "Morality and the Novel." *Twentieth Century Literary Criticism.* Ed. David Lodge. London: Longman, 1972. 127-131.

—————. "The spirit of place." *Twentieth Century Criticism.* Ed. David Lodge. London: Longman, 1972. 122-127.

—————. "Why the novel matters." *Twentieth Century*

Criticism. Ed. David Lodge. London: Longman, 1972. 131-135.

Lewis, Pramila. "Of the Oppressed lot." *Patriot*. 4 March 1990, 10.

Linton, Ralph. "Cultural and Personality Factors Affecting Economic Growth." *The Progress of Underdeveloped Areas*. Ed. Bert F. Hoselitz. Chicago: University of Chicago Press, 1952. 83-84.

Lubbock, Percy. *The Craft of Fiction*. New Delhi: B.I. Publications, 1979.

Lukacs, Georg. "The ideology of modernism." *Twentieth Century Literary Criticism*. Ed. David Lodge. London: Longman, 1972. 474-488.

Mahajan, Vidyadhar. *History of India*. New Delhi: S. Chand and Company, 1985.

Mandelbaum, David G. "The Family in India." *The Family: Its Fiction and Destiny*. Ed. Ruth Anshen. New York: Harper and Brothers, 1949. 92-102.

Miller, Arthur. *Arthur Miller's Collected Plays*. New York: The Viking Press, 1957.

Moffatt, Michael. *An Untouchable Community in South India: Structure and Consensus*. New York: Princeton University Press, 1979.

Murthy, U.R. Anantha. *Samskara*. Trans. A.K. Ramanujam. Delhi: Oxford University Press, 1978.

Naipaul, V.S. *An Area of Darkness*. London: Penguin, 1968.

——————. *Mr. Stone and the Knights Companion*. London: Penguin Books, 1973.

Narasimhan, Shakuntala. "Shadows in the Countryside." *Indian Express*. 5 April 1987: 20.

Orwell, George. "Politics and the English language." *Twentieth Century Literary Criticism*. Ed. David Lodge. London: Longman, 1972. 360-370.

Pandurangan, Prema. "Juxtaposition and Contraposition." The *Hindu*. 3 May 1979: 21.

Raghavacharyulu, D.V.K. "The Task Ahead." *Critical Essays on Indian Writing in English*. Ed. M.K. Naik, S.K. Desai, G.S. Amur. Dharwar: Karnatak University, 1968. 337-344.

Ravindranathan, S. "Quest for Justice: A Reading of Romen Basu's *Outcast* and *Blackstone*." *The Journal of Life, Art and Literature*. 3.1 (July 1992): 1-13.

——————. *Principles of Literary Criticism*. Nagercoil: Rohini Agencies, 1993.

Ross, Aileen D. *The Hindu Family in its Urban Setting*. Delhi: Oxford University Press, 1973.

Sartre, Jean Paul. "Why Write?" *Twentieth Century Literary Criticism*. Ed. David Lodge. London: Longman, 1972. 371-385.

Scott, Wilbur. "Introduction." *Five Approaches of Literary Criticism*. Ed. Wilbur Scott. New York: Collier Books, 1962.

Sharma, O.P. "Trans-Cultural Panorama." *The Tribune*. 25 October 1980. 7.

Shaw, Bernard. "Candida." *The Complete Plays of Bernard Shaw*. London: Odhams Press Ltd., n.d.

——————. "The Devil's Disciple." *The Complete Plays of Bernard Shaw*. London: Odhams Press Ltd., n.d.

Singh, Anand Raj. "Novel with Social Purpose. "*The Pioneer*. 10 May 1987.

Singh, Khushwant. *Train to Pakistan*. Delhi: Ravi Dayal Publisher, 1988.

Singh, R.S. *Indian Novel in English*. New Delhi: Arnold-Heinemann, 1977.

Singh, Veena. "Reality and Revolution?" *Indian Books Chronicle* (May-July 1987): 151.

Tagore, Rabindranath. "Chandalika." *Three Plays*. trans. Marjorie Sykes. Calcutta: Macmillan, 1950.

Tennyson, Alfred Lord. "Ulysses." *English Verse*. London: Oxford University Press, Vol. V, 1963.

Vatsa, Rajendra Singh. *The Depressed Classes of India*. New Delhi: Gitanjali Prakashan, 1977.

Wallace, Richard Cheever and Wendy Drew Wallace. *Sociology*. Boston: Allyn and Bacon Inc., 1985.

Walsh, William. *Indian Literature in English*. London: Longman, 1990.

Wellek, Rene and Austin Warren. *Theory of Literature*. Middleton: Penguin, 1956.

Williams, Raymond. "Realism and the Contemporary Novel." *Twentieth Century Literary Criticism*. Ed. David Lodge. London: Longman, 1972. 581-592.

Wilson, Edmund. "Marxism and Literature." *Twentieth Century Literary Criticism*. Ed. David Lodge. London: Longman, 1972. 241-252.

Index